VOLKER HINZ

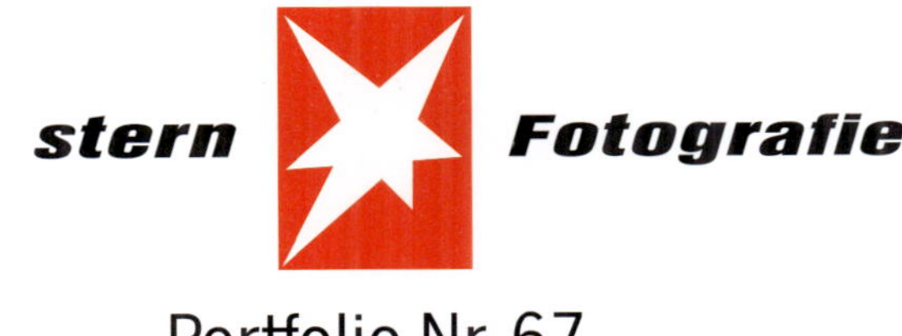

Portfolio Nr. 67

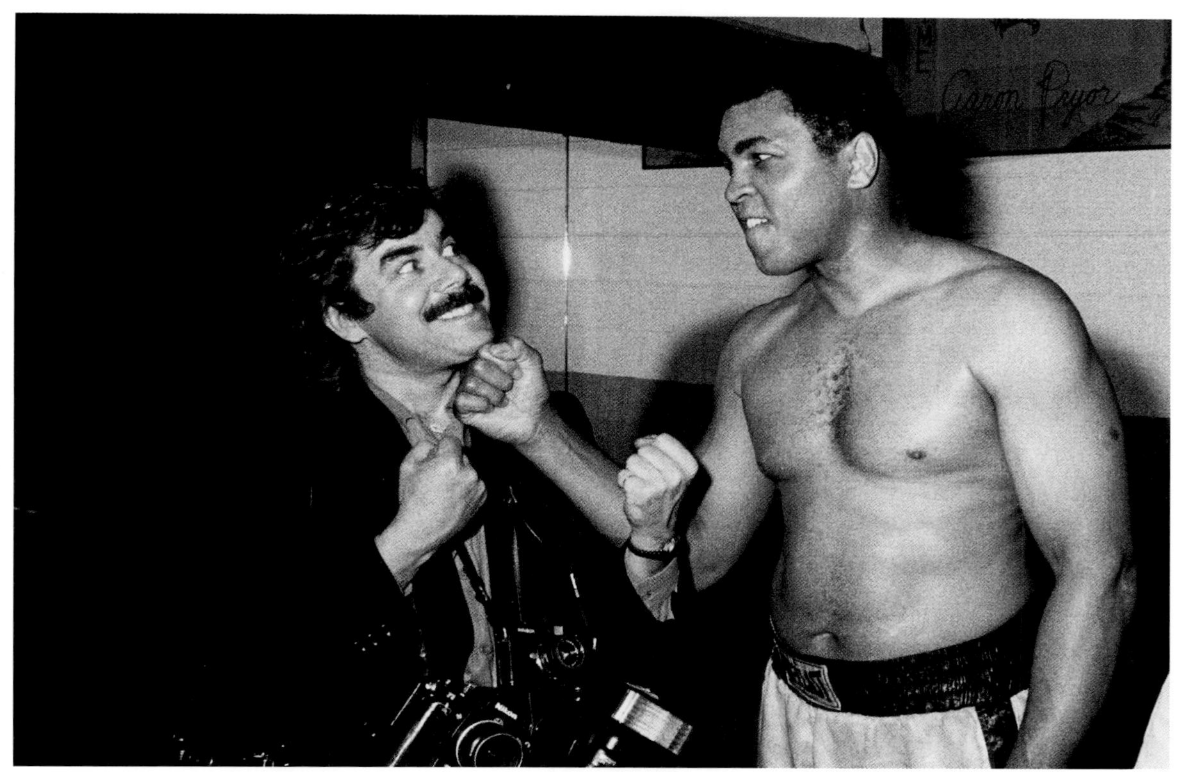

Volker Hinz und Muhammad Ali 1984 in Santa Monica, Kalifornien

Liebe *stern*-FOTOGRAFIE-Leser,

Einmal angenommen, dieses Vorwort wäre ein Foto und Volker Hinz hätte es fotografiert. Dann würden wir hinschauen, und das Bild würde uns begeistern, weil Hinz fast immer etwas schafft, was kein Text in dieser Kürze, in dieser Präzision vermag: Volker Hinz formt in seinen Aufnahmen aus zwei Gegensätzen fast immer etwas Drittes, oftmals Unbeschreibliches.

Seine Aufnahmen sind Schnappschüsse und zugleich Gemälde, seine Beobachtungen charmant zurückhaltend und gleichsam unerbittlich nah. Volker Hinz ist stets in Bewegung und strahlt doch eine enorme Ruhe und Souveränität aus. Das mag damit zu tun haben, dass Volker Hinz seit nunmehr fast vier Jahrzehnten für den *stern* fotografiert. Seine Sicht auf Dinge und Menschen prägt bis heute die Anmutung dieser Zeitschrift. Und umgekehrt hat sich auch die journalistische Seele des *stern* tief eingeschrieben in die Haltung und Arbeitsweise unseres Kollegen. Das fotografische Werk von Volker Hinz veranschaulicht die optische Vielfalt und inhaltliche Kraft des *stern*, seinen Charme und seine Leidenschaft.

Volker Hinz ist ein Boxer, der mit Samthandschuhen kämpft. Er tänzelt, den Kopf in der Luft, beide Beine stets dort, wo sie hingehören: auf dem Boden. Hinz kennt alle Tricks und jeden Ring. Er weiß fast alles, aber niemals etwas besser. „Float like a butterfly, sting like a bee." Jenes Credo, das der Boxer Muhammad Ali, den Volker Hinz im Jahr 1984 drei Tage für den *stern* begleitete, einst formulierte, gilt auch für seine Arbeit. Eigenschaften, die Volker Hinz zu einem der sympathischsten und unterhaltsamsten Chronisten unserer Zeit gemacht haben.

Dear *stern* FOTOGRAFIE Reader,

Just imagine this editorial was a photograph and Volker Hinz had shot it. We would look at it and get the wow effect, because Volker Hinz nearly always manages to achieve something no text of this length is capable of with such precision. Out of two contrasts Volker Hinz almost always creates a third, often indescribable, element in his photographs. They are both snapshots and pictures, and his observations are both charmingly reserved and relentlessly intimate. Although Volker Hinz is always on the move, he still radiates a powerful sense of calm and assuredness. That may have something to do with the fact that he has been taking photographs for *stern* for nearly four decades. His perspective on people and things has shaped the look of this magazine, while at the same time, the journalistic soul of *stern* has become deeply inscribed in our colleague's attitude and the way he works. Volker Hinz' photographic oeuvre illustrates the visual diversity and substantive power of this magazine, as well as its charm and passion. Volker Hinz is a boxer who fights with velvet gloves. He bobs and weaves, head in the air but both feet firmly on the ground, where they belong. Volker Hinz knows all the tricks and every ring. He knows almost everything, but never knows anything better. "Float like a butterfly, sting like a bee": what was once the credo of Muhammad Ali – the boxer Volker Hinz spent three days photographing for *stern* in 1984 – applies to Hinz' work, too. Such qualities have made Volker Hinz one of the most likeable and entertaining chroniclers of our day and age.

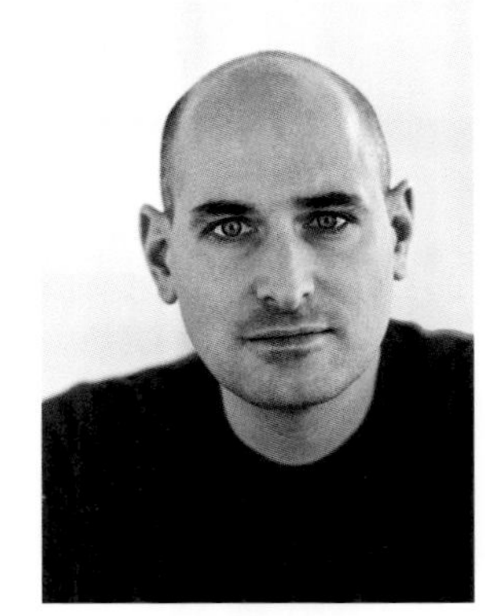

**Dominik Wichmann,
stellvertretender
stern-Chefredakteur**

DER SANFTMÜTIGE FALKE

Aus Fotos Erlebnisse zu machen ist die Kunst und das Handwerk von Volker Hinz. Fast 40 Jahre fotografiert er für den *stern*, seine Bilder sind längst Fotografiegeschichte. Im Großen wie im Kleinen

Turning photos into real experiences is the art and craft of Volker Hinz. For almost 40 years he has been shooting photos for *stern* and his pictures – both large and small – made photographic history long ago

Von/By Jochen Siemens

Volker Hinz und sein Sohn Theodor Hinz in Hamburg
Volker Hinz and his son Theodor Hinz in Hamburg

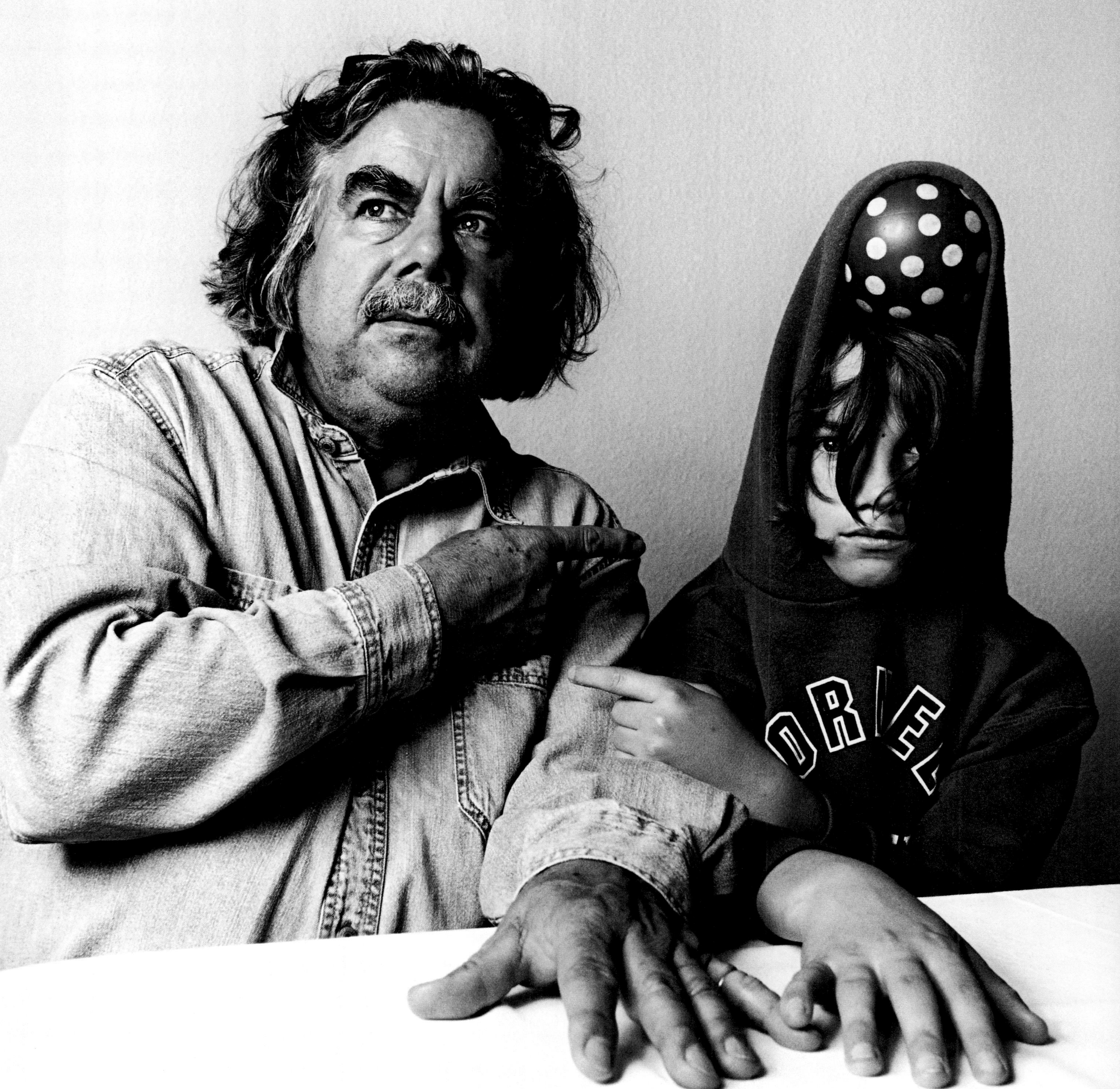

Wenn man ihn fragt, ob ihm schon einmal ein Bild entwischt sei, so wie ein fliehendes Reh auf einer Lichtung dem Jäger, den es gewittert hat, erzählt Volker Hinz eine Geschichte. Neulich war das, sagt er, da sprach Altkanzler Helmut Schmidt in einer Halle, und danach schob man ihn in seinem Rollstuhl in einen Pausenraum dieser Halle. „Ich bin natürlich mit und als Erster in das Zimmer gegangen. Als Erster ist wichtig, dann können sie einen nicht so leicht rausschmeißen. Ich war wie immer höflich, habe Schmidt Kaffee eingeschenkt, Zucker geholt und Milch. Gute Stimmung ist entscheidend. Aber genau in dem Moment, als ich die Milch holte, nahm er seinen Gehstock in die Hand und zog damit den Aschenbecher von der anderen Seite des Tisches zu sich herüber. Das war das Foto. Und ich habe es nicht gemacht, weil ich die Milch in der Hand hatte."

Es ist eine kleine Geschichte eines entwischten Bildes, aber sie erzählt viel über einen großen Fotografen. Es ist nicht die Geschichte von Belichtungszeit, Weitwinkel oder Filmrollen, sondern die Geschichte vom Gespür. „Die Fotoreportage", sagte einmal Henri Cartier-Bresson, „verlangt eine Zusammenarbeit von Intellekt, Auge und Herz." Gespür eben. Und wer Volker Hinz kennt, wer schon einmal neben ihm gestanden oder sich mit ihm durch dichtes Gedränge geschoben hat, wer also schon einmal mit ihm Bilder gesucht hat, der konnte zusehen, wie Intellekt, Auge und Herz dann in seinem ganzen Körper arbeiten. Die Kamera? Die kommt zum Schluss, die ist immer an Volker Hinz festgewachsen, und es gibt Momente, da macht das eine Auge das Foto und das andere sucht schon das nächste. Aber vorher ist das Gespür, das Wissen um das Timing: als Erster in einem Raum sein, das fotografische Geschehen erwarten und ihm nicht hinterherlaufen. Und es ist die Fähigkeit, der Luft solcher Räume die Anspannung des Fotografischen, die Gewalt der Kamera zu nehmen, abzulenken, Kaffee auszuschenken, nicht zu lauern, sondern sich zu bewegen. „Die Welt ist in Bewegung, und man darf gegenüber einer beweglichen Sache nicht in Bewegungslosigkeit verharren", so nannte es der große Cartier-Bresson.

Volker Hinz ist ein deutscher Fotograf, und das „deutsch" ist wichtig, weil Hinz seit über 40 Jahren so etwas wie eines der Augen dieses Landes ist. Das waren und sind andere auch, Robert Lebeck, Thomas Hoepker oder Josef „Jupp" Darchinger zum Beispiel, aber jeder von ihnen hatte und hat eine andere fotografische Handschrift. Wenn man heute eine Turnhalle mit den wichtigsten ihrer Fotografien aushängen würde – und es sind Tausende –, ergäbe das ein Museum der deutschen Blicke und Anblicke der vergangenen 40 oder mehr Jahre. Und es ist egal, wie durchgemischt man alle diese Fotos hängen würde, die Hinz'sche Handschrift wäre sofort zu erkennen. Weil es gespürte Bilder sind. Hinz selbst mag es nicht so gern, wenn man ihn nach einem deutschen Blick fragt, dazu hat er viel zu intensiv in die Werke großer Meister wie Cartier-Bresson oder W. Eugene Smith geblickt, wenn sie auch nie seine Lehrer waren. Sein Lehrer war Hinz selbst. Und Deutschland. Damals und heute.

Vielleicht liegt es daran, dass er an einem Flussufer geboren wurde. 1947 war das, in Hamburg-Blankenese, in einem dieser Häuser, die direkt am Elbhang liegen und aus deren Fenstern man immer den Fluss und die Schiffe sehen kann, die in die Welt fahren. Auf einen Fluss zu blicken heißt, sehen zu lernen, vorne das Ufer, in der Mitte die Schiffe

Ask Volker Hinz if he's ever missed a picture, like a deer that takes flight on getting wind of the hunter, and he tells you a story. Not long ago, he says, ex-Chancellor Helmut Schmidt was giving a talk in a hall and when he had finished, he was pushed into a side room in his wheelchair. "Of course I went with him and was actually first into the room. Getting in first is always vital because then they can't throw you out so easily. Polite as ever, I poured some coffee into Schmidt's cup and went to get him some sugar and milk. After all, a good mood is decisive. But just as I was getting the milk, he took hold of his walking stick and used it to drag over the ashtray from the other side of the table. That would have been the photo! And I missed it because I was holding the milk."

It may be only a little story about a missed photo, but it tells us a lot about a great photographer. It's not a story about exposure times, wide-angle cameras or rolls of film, but a story about intuition. "Photojournalism," Henri Cartier-Bresson once said, "demands collaboration between head, heart and eye." That's one way of describing intuition. If you know Volker Hinz, have stood next to him, pushed your way through a crowd with him or picked out pictures with him, you can see how head, heart and eye are working throughout his body. The camera? That comes last, attached to him like a limpet. There are moments when one eye is taking a photo and the other one is already looking for the next shot. But before that comes intuition, and the knowledge that you've got to be the first in a room so you can wait for a photograph to happen, and not end up running after it. And it's his ability to take the photographic tension out of the atmosphere in such rooms, the brute force of the camera, by sidetracking somebody, pouring a cup of coffee and moving around instead of lying in wait. As the great Cartier-Bresson once said, "The world is in motion so you can't stay motionless when you're faced with something on the move."

Volker Hinz is a German photographer, and the German bit is important because for more than 40 years, Hinz has been one of the eyes of this country. There were, and are, others – Robert Lebeck, Thomas Hoepker or Josef "Jupp" Darchinger for example – but each one of them had or has a different photographic signature. If you filled a hall with their most important photographs – and there are thousands of them – it would be a museum of German views and sights from the past four decades or more. And however much you mixed up the photos, Hinz' signature would be immediately recognizable – because his are intuitive pictures. Hinz himself doesn't like to be asked about his German view of things. After all, he has looked much too intensively into the works of great masters like Cartier-Bresson or W. Eugene Smith. But they were never his teachers. He was his own teacher – along with the country of his birth, past and present.

Maybe it's because he was born on the banks of a river in 1947, in a house on the northern flank of the River Elbe in the Hamburg district of Blankenese. From there you can see the river and ships bound for des-

Volker Hinz mit dem Autor William S. Burroughs in Lawrence, Kansas, 1987
Volker Hinz with the writer William S. Burroughs in Lawrence, Kansas, 1987

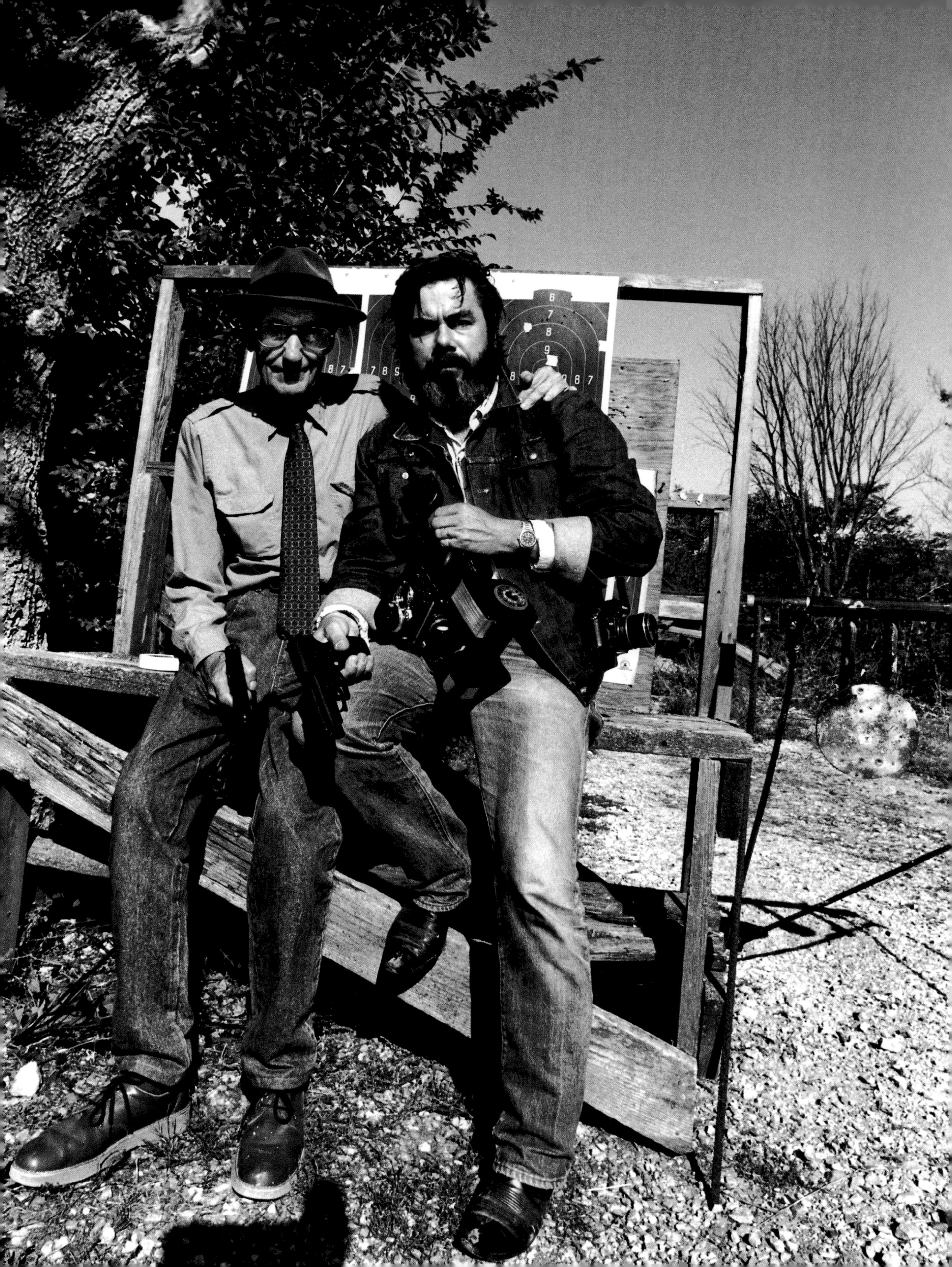

und weiter hinten das Land. Räume zu sehen heißt, Träume zu sehen. Hinz' Vater war Goldschmied, seine Mutter Buchhalterin, es war, wie er sagt, eine schöne Kindheit am Fluss einer großen Stadt. Nach der Schule machte Hinz 1963 eine Lehre als Elektronikmechaniker beim Hamburger Flugzeugbau, es interessierte ihn, und „es klang nach Zukunft". Die Fotografie kam erst in Sicht, als Hinz nach der Lehre zur Bundeswehr musste, damals noch 18 Monate, und in einer Kaserne in Rendsburg die Ödheit des Wacheschiebens erlebte und sich in solchen Nächten mit einem Fotografen anfreundete. „Das hat mich interessiert, Verschlusszeiten, Blenden, Objektive und daraus Bilder zu machen", sagt er. Die erste Kamera war eine kompakte Edixa Reflex des Herstellers Wirgin mit Tuchschlitzverschluss, „seitdem habe ich nie wieder aufgehört zu fotografieren".

Es kam ein Impuls hinzu, den die meisten Fotografen bei ihren ersten Bildern verspüren, über den sie aber, wie auch Hinz, nur sparsam Auskunft geben. In den 60er Jahren war Fotografieren ein ungleich komplizierteres Unterfangen als heute – man brauchte die Kenntnis der Technik, der Objektive, des Lichtes, dazu eine Dunkelkammer mit Chemikalien, Geduld und Hoffnung, wenn das Bild auf dem Abzug im Entwicklerbad zur Welt kam. Das konnten nicht viele, und wer es konnte, hatte bald das – wenn auch noch nicht glamouröse – Ansehen eines Bildlieferanten. Und dass sie liefern mussten, gab Fotografen immer einen Anlass, dort anwesend zu sein, wo sie sein wollten. Sie standen nicht wie Gaffer herum, sie hatten sich nicht verlaufen, und sie mussten sich nicht entschuldigen. Der amerikanische Fotograf Bruce Weber sagte einmal, die Fotografie habe ihm über seine Schüchternheit hinweggeholfen, „weil ich immer einen Grund hatte, auf Menschen zuzugehen. Ich wollte ein Foto." Volker Hinz nickt, wenn man ihm das erzählt. Nur die Schüchternheit, die habe er heute nicht mehr, sagt er.

Noch in der Kaserne beschließt Hinz, Fotograf zu werden. Er fährt auf politische Versammlungen, auf Parteitage und andere Anlässe, zu denen sich Menschen öffentlich zeigen. Und fotografiert. Nicht sehr groß, aber von energischer Statur mit damals längeren schwarzen Haaren und einem Schnauzbart, ist Volker Hinz bald der Fotograf, der immer da ist und dessen Bilder die Zeitungen kaufen. Man fängt an, ihn zu kennen. Und zu verfluchen, weil Volker Hinz aus dem fotografischen „nahe" ein „ganz nahe" machte, wie auf dem SPD-Parteitag 1971, über den der Fotograf Hanns Hubmann später spottete: „Ohne Hinz kein Brandt." Es gab kein einziges Bild des Parteivorsitzenden ohne einen Hinz daneben, davor oder dahinter. Hinz selbst sagt, dass er damals lernte, sich zu bewegen und die Bewegungen anderer zu lesen. Und das ist bis heute eines seiner, wenn man so will, Betriebsgeheimnisse geblieben. Er kennt die ritualisierte Körpersprache von Politikern und anderen Prominenten auswendig. Er weiß schon, wohin die Hand geht, wenn ein Gerhard Schröder anfängt, sie zu bewegen, oder mit welchem Timbre in den Augen Angela Merkel gleich blicken wird, wenn sie einen schwergewichtigen Satz mit „Ich persönlich glaube ..." anfängt. Einer wie Hinz kennt das Bild schon, wenn es noch gar nicht in Sicht ist.

Und er weiß, dass wer ein Foto anschaut, einen Raum sehen muss. Einen Vordergrund, eine Mitte und einen Hintergrund. So wie damals an der Elbe. Bilder wirken dann, wenn man in sie hineinschauen kann wie in ein Leben, und nicht auf ihnen herumblicken muss wie auf einer Fläche – Fotoschule der klassischsten Art, leider heute oft verblichen.

tinations all over the world. Looking out onto a river teaches you how to look: in the foreground the riverbank, in the middle the ships, and beyond them the land on the other side. And seeing spaces means seeing dreams. Hinz' father was a goldsmith, his mother a bookkeeper. He says he enjoyed his childhood in the flux of a big city. After leaving school in 1963, Hinz started an apprenticeship at a Hamburg aircraft manufacturer. It interested him and "sounded like it had a future". Photography only came into view after he had finished his apprenticeship and was doing 18 months of military service in the German Army. Night-time guard duty at the barracks in Rendsburg was utterly boring but it was then that he made friends with a photographer. "I got interested in shutter speeds, apertures, lenses and making pictures out of all that," he says. His first camera was a compact Wirgin Edixa Reflex with a fabric focal-plane shutter. "Since then, I've never stopped taking photos."

And there was also a certain impulse of the kind most photographers feel when they take their first pictures, and one they are reluctant to talk about. Hinz is no exception. In the 1960s, photography was a significantly more complicated business than it is today. You needed to know all about the technology, lenses, lighting and darkroom chemicals. And you needed patience and hope when waiting for the picture to appear in the developing tank. Not many people had all these skills, and those who did had the looks of image providers, back then still a far from glamorous profession. Because they had to deliver the goods, photographers always had a reason for being where they were. They didn't just stand around gaping. They hadn't lost their way. They didn't have to excuse themselves for being in a particular place at a particular time. The American photographer Bruce Weber once said that photography had helped him to overcome his shyness "because I always had a good reason for going up to people – I wanted a photo". Volker Hinz nods in agreement. But the shyness has gone, he says.

It was back in those barrack-room days that Hinz decided to become a photographer. He went to political meetings, party conventions and other events where people presented themselves to the public. And he took photos. Not tall but with an energetic figure and, in those days, long black hair and a moustache, Volker Hinz soon became the photographer who was always around and sold his pictures to newspapers. People began to notice him, and flee from him because Hinz turned the close-up of photography into an ultra-close-up. After the Social Democrats' party convention in 1971, another photographer, Hanns Hubmann, scoffed: "No Brandt without Hinz". No photo of the party chairman Willy Brandt was seen without Hinz standing behind, beside or in front of him. Hinz himself says that it was then that he learnt how to move around and read other people's movements. This has remained one of his trade secrets, so to speak. He knows the ritualized body language of politicians and other VIPs. He senses where Gerhard Schröder's hand will go once it starts to move, and what expression there will be in Angela Merkel's eyes when she starts a sentence with "Personally I think ...". Someone like Volker Hinz knows a picture before it's even in view.

And he knows that everyone who looks at a photo has to see space – foreground, middle and background. Just like it was on the River Elbe. Pictures impact when you can look into them, like into a real life, and not when you have to look over them like on a surface. Fundamentals of photography, but unfortunately frequently faded ones nowadays. Volker Hinz uses little technical tricks to create such spaces: a wide-angle lens held at eye level and pointing slightly downwards so that lines or frames can be seen; shifting the centre of a landscape-format picture to the left or right because magazines have a gutter in the middle that can destroy a picture; or his portrait of Woody Allen, seemingly a fast job in maybe just two minutes. Woody Allen is looking into the camera and Hinz tells him to hold his hand in front of his mouth, but at

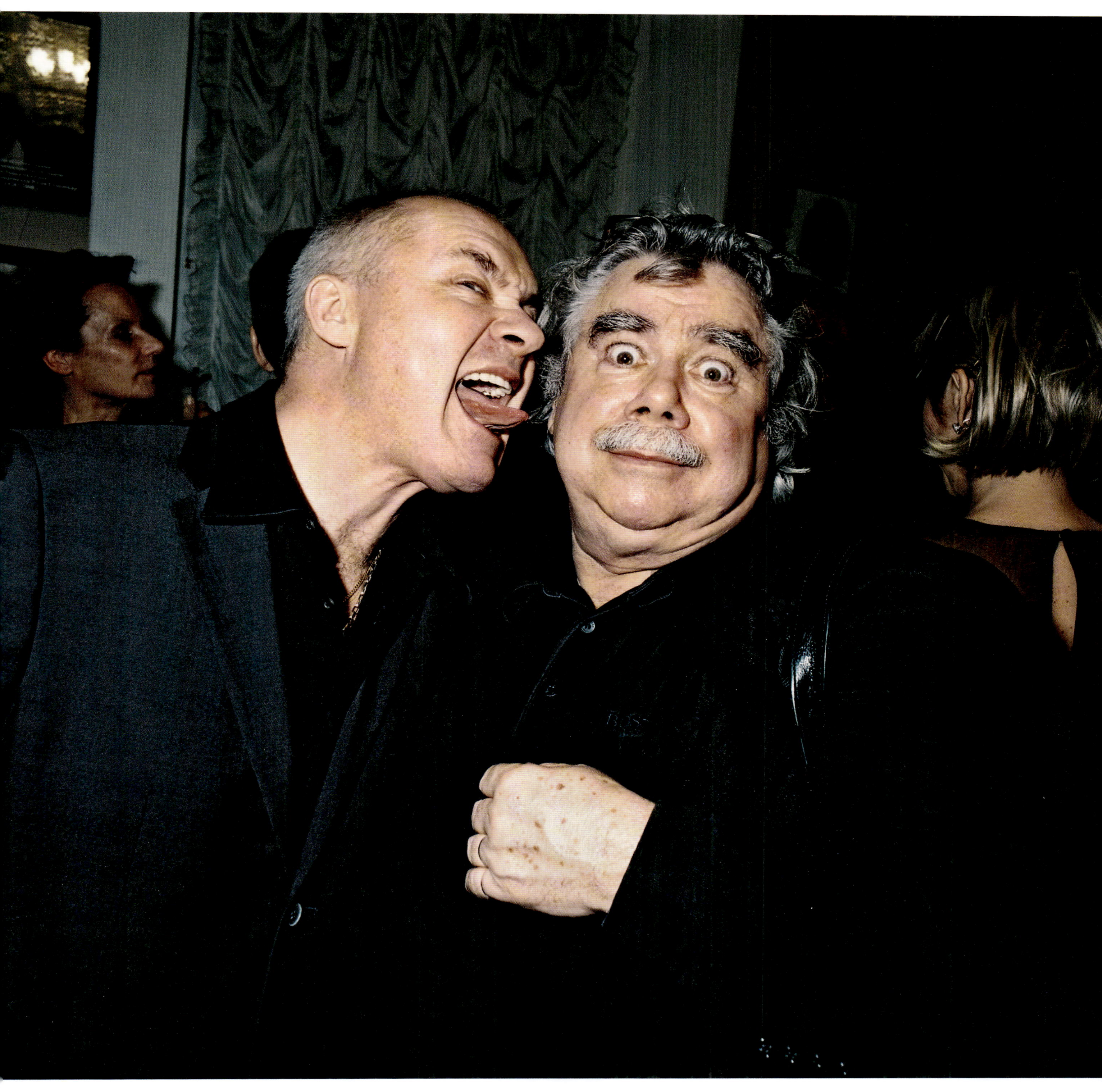

Falkenauge: Volker Hinz mit dem Künstler Damien Hirst in Kiew, 2010
A hawk's eye: Volker Hinz with the artist Damien Hirst in Kiev, 2010

Biografie

Es sind kleine technische Tricks, mit denen Volker Hinz diese Räume herstellen kann: Weitwinkelobjektiv aus Augenhöhe leicht nach unten gehalten, damit Linien oder Rahmen zu sehen sind. Das Zentrum des Bildes bei einem Querformat immer leicht nach links oder rechts schieben, weil Zeitschriften in der Mitte einen sogenannten „Bruch" bei der Heftung haben, der ein Bild zerstören kann. Oder zum Beispiel sein Woody Allen, ein augenscheinlich schnelles Porträt, zwei Minuten Zeit vielleicht. Allen blickt in die Kamera, und Hinz sagt, „die Hand einmal vor den Mund, aber im rechten Winkel". Vordergrund: die Hand; Bildmitte: das Gesicht; Hintergrund: eine weiße Wand.

Das war später, aber schon Volker Hinz' erste Bilder machten den Fotografen Sven Simon, Sohn des Verlegers Axel Springer, Anfang der 70er Jahre auf den mit dem Schnauzbart aufmerksam. Sie waren wie die der anderen, aber besser. Dichter und gespürter. Es war eine, noch ungestüme, Handschrift, die Simon für seine junge Agentur brauchte, und so machte er Hinz Anfang der 70er Jahre zum Büroleiter seiner Bonner Dependance. Bonn, Brandt, Barzel, Wehner – die Macht in der Provinz. Volker Hinz war immer überall, irgendwie. „Barzel sagte mir an einem Nachmittag leise, ich solle mal im Parlamentssaal bleiben und ihm folgen, wenn er gehe, mehr nicht. Also folgte ich ihm, als er den Saal verließ und allein ins Bundestagsrestaurant ging. Niemand sonst war da. Nur Barzel und Brandt, die sich zu einem Bier trafen, der Kanzler und sein Gegner. Ich hatte das Foto. Nicht sehr dicht dran, aber die Entfernung machte es besser." Eine von vielen Geschichten, die Hinz aus der Bonner Zeit erzählen kann.

Doch er war unruhig und wollte weiter. Der *stern*, das große Reportagemagazin in Hamburg, war der Magnet, zu dem er sich hingezogen fühlte. Sie hatten dort schon viele seiner Bilder gedruckt, dann, 1974, kam der Anruf: „Hinz, wir brauchen einen Fotoreporter wie dich." „Nicht viele Kunststückchen machen, sondern die richtigen, wichtigen Bildern, das sollen unsere Fotoreporter. Der *stern* muss aggressiv sein", sagte ihm damals Rolf Gillhausen, das richtende Auge des Magazins. Hinz nickt noch heute, wenn er das hört. Volker Hinz ist bis 2012 beim *stern* geblieben, einige Jahre davon als Reporter in New York, die anderen im Rest der Welt und immer wieder in Deutschland. Unter seinen Bildern finden sich unzählige Klassiker, über die man nur zwei, drei Worte sagen muss, und gleich hat sie jeder vor Augen. „Beckenbauer und Pelé unter der Dusche" zum Beispiel. Wieder so ein Schuss, den keiner hat, aufgenommen im Duschraum der Cosmos-New-York-Mannschaft, wo Beckenbauer und Pelé Ende der 70er Jahre spielten. Ein damals unerhört intimes Bild zweier nackter Weltfußballer mit Seife in den Haaren. „Ich habe noch zu Beckenbauer gesagt, er soll sich ein bisschen von der Kamera wegdrehen, damit nicht alles zu sehen ist", erzählt Hinz und beschreibt damit wieder sein Gespür dafür, wie man sogar von einem großen Star ein Nacktfoto machen kann, das selbst der bis heute mag.

Hört man heute Fotochefs und Artdirectoren über Volker Hinz sprechen, fällt ihnen meist das wehmütige Wort vom „letzten Alleskönner mit der Kamera" oder Ähnliches ein. Ein bisschen ist es so, weil sich die Zeiten geändert haben und es kaum noch Zeitschriften mit einem eigenen Stall selbstbewusster Fotografen gibt. Ein bisschen ist es aber auch so, weil genau jene, die das mit Wehmut sagen, die Kunst und das Handwerk einer, sagen wir, Hinz'schen Schule immer weniger suchen. Gespür und Atmosphäre zu erzeugen kann man nicht bestellen und nicht digitalisieren. Man muss es mit der Kamera leben. Und wenn man es einmal kann, dann bekommt man Muhammad Ali dazu, vor der Kamera zu schlafen, William S. Burroughs, mit einer Pistole herumzulaufen, Anna Netrebko, ihre Zunge zu rollen, und Kate Moss, ihre Füße in Goldfarbe zu tauchen. Anders gesagt: alles fotografieren zu können und danach dem Zuschauer nicht nur ein Bild zu liefern, sondern das, was Fotografie kann – Erleben. „Jeder von uns", sagt Cartier-Bresson, „braucht Samthandschuhe und Falkenaugen." Samthandschuhe und Falkenaugen: Besser kann man Volker Hinz nicht beschreiben.

right angles: in the foreground his hand, in the middle of the picture his mouth, and in the background a wall he is leaning against.

That photo came later, but it was his early pictures that caught the eye of another photographer, Sven Simon, the son of the publisher Axel Springer. Hinz' photos were like those of other photographers, only better – closer and more intuitive. It was the somewhat impetuous signature Simon needed for his newly established agency, and he hired Hinz as the head of his Bonn office in the early 1970s. Bonn, Brandt, Barzel, Wehner – men of power in a small provincial town on the Rhine. And Volker Hinz was somehow omnipresent. "One afternoon, Barzel whispered to me that I should stay in the parliamentary chamber and follow him when he leaves. That was all. So I followed him when he left and went into the Bundestag restaurant on his own. Nobody else was there, and then Barzel met Brandt for a beer – the chancellor and his opponent. I had the photo, not that much of a close-up, but a certain amount of distance made it a better one." Just one of the many stories Hinz can relate from those Bonn days.

But he was anxious to move on and up. *stern*, the great photojournalistic magazine based in Hamburg, had a magnetic appeal for Hinz and had already printed plenty of his pictures. The phone call finally came in 1974: "Hinz, we need a photojournalist like you." Back then, Rolf Gillhausen, the regulatory eye of the magazine, had this to say: "Our photojournalists shouldn't go for lots of stunts but for the right, the important pictures, because *stern* is aggressive." Hinz still nods today when he hears that quote. Volker Hinz stayed with *stern* till 2012. He spent some years working as a photo-reporter in New York and most of the time in other parts of the world, interrupted by frequent spells in Germany. His life work includes numerous classic photos. Describe them in a couple of words and most people can see the photo in their mind's eye: "Beckenbauer and Pelé in the shower", for example – one of the shots nobody else has done, taken in a shower room of the Cosmos New York team where Beckenbauer and Pelé played in the late 1970s. At that time it was an outrageously intimate photo of two of the world's best footballers standing naked under the shower with soap in their hair. "I told Beckenbauer to turn away from the camera a bit so you wouldn't see everything," Hinz recalls and again reveals the intuition with which he was able to make a nude photo of a great star, which the latter still likes to this day.

When picture editors and art directors talk about Volker Hinz, they come up with wistful comments like "the last of the all-rounders with a camera". That is true to a certain extent because times have changed and there are hardly any magazines with their own stable of self-assured photographers. But it is also true because the very people who wistfully say such things are less and less interested in the art and craft of what we might call the Hinz school of photography. The art of intuition and atmosphere is not something you can simply have to order or even digitalize. You have to live it out with the camera. But if you've got these skills, you can get Muhammed Ali to sleep in front of a camera, William S. Burroughs to run round with a gun, Anna Netrebko to roll her tongue and Kate Moss to dip her feet in gold paint. Or put differently, the ability to photograph anything and everything and then offer the viewer not just a picture but what photography is capable of – an experience. "A velvet hand, a hawk's eye," Cartier-Bresson once said, "these we should all have." A velvet hand and a hawk's eye – there's no better way of describing Volker Hinz.

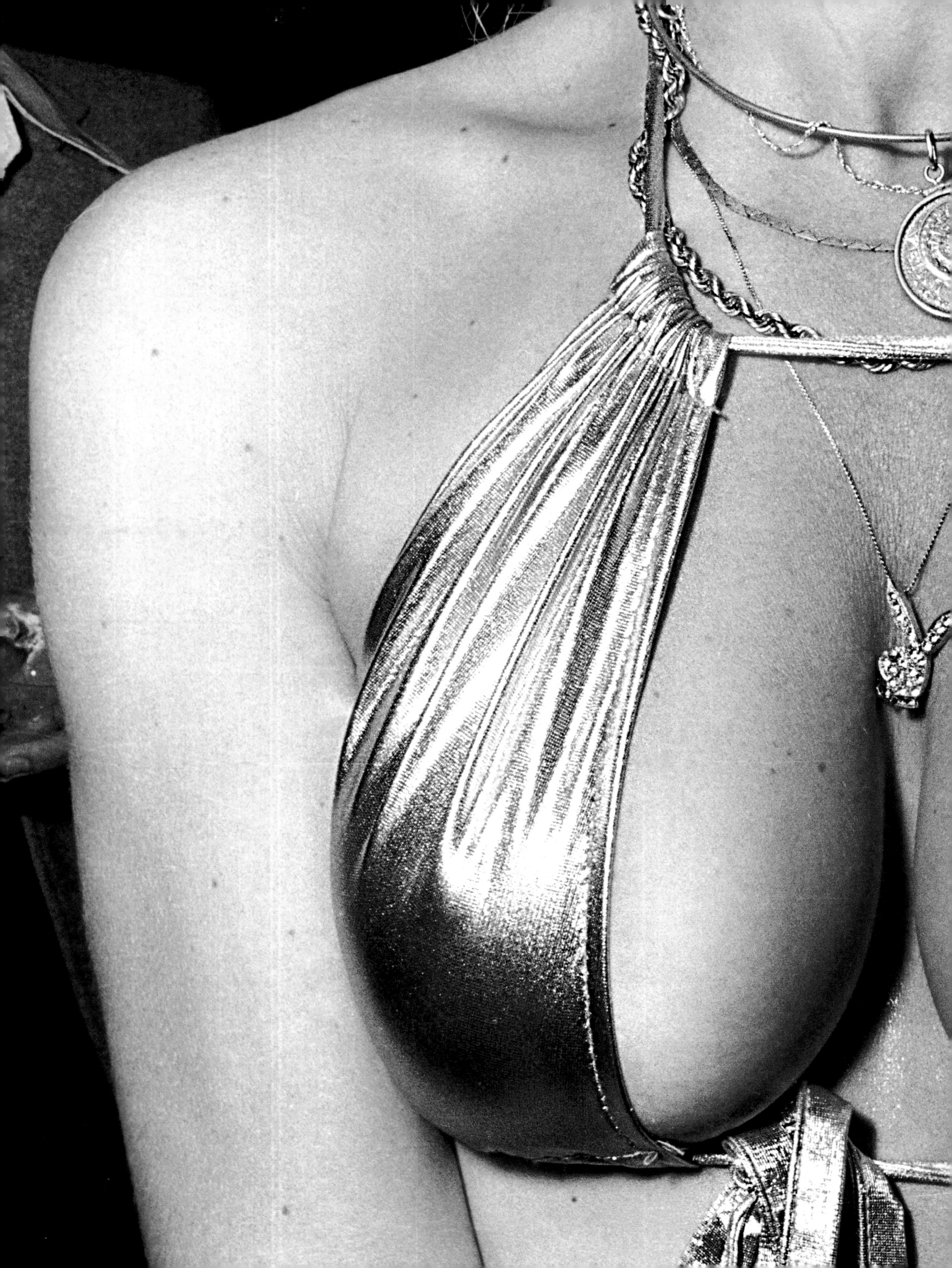

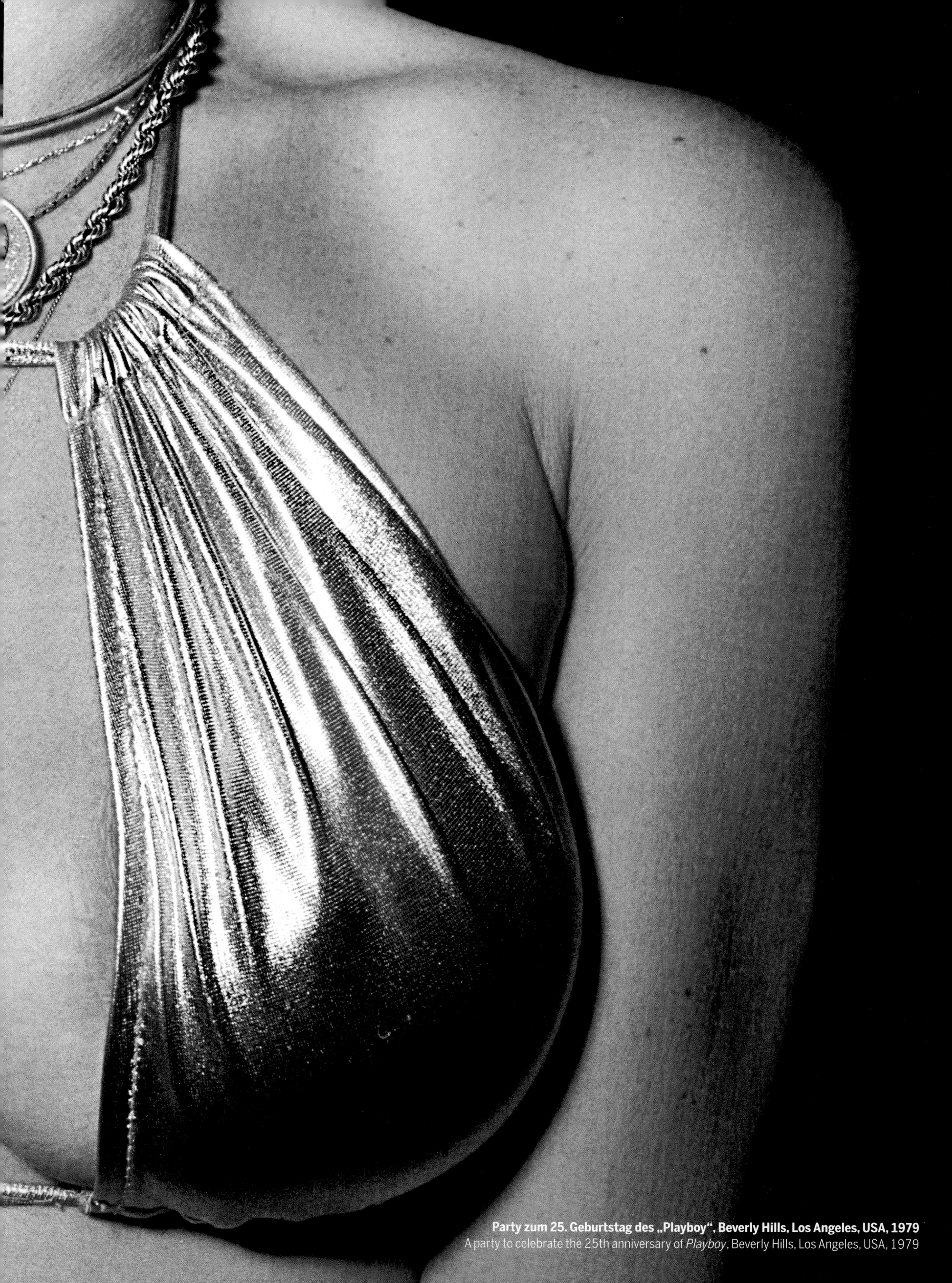

Party zum 25. Geburtstag des „Playboy", Beverly Hills, Los Angeles, USA, 1979
A party to celebrate the 25th anniversary of *Playboy*, Beverly Hills, Los Angeles, USA, 1979

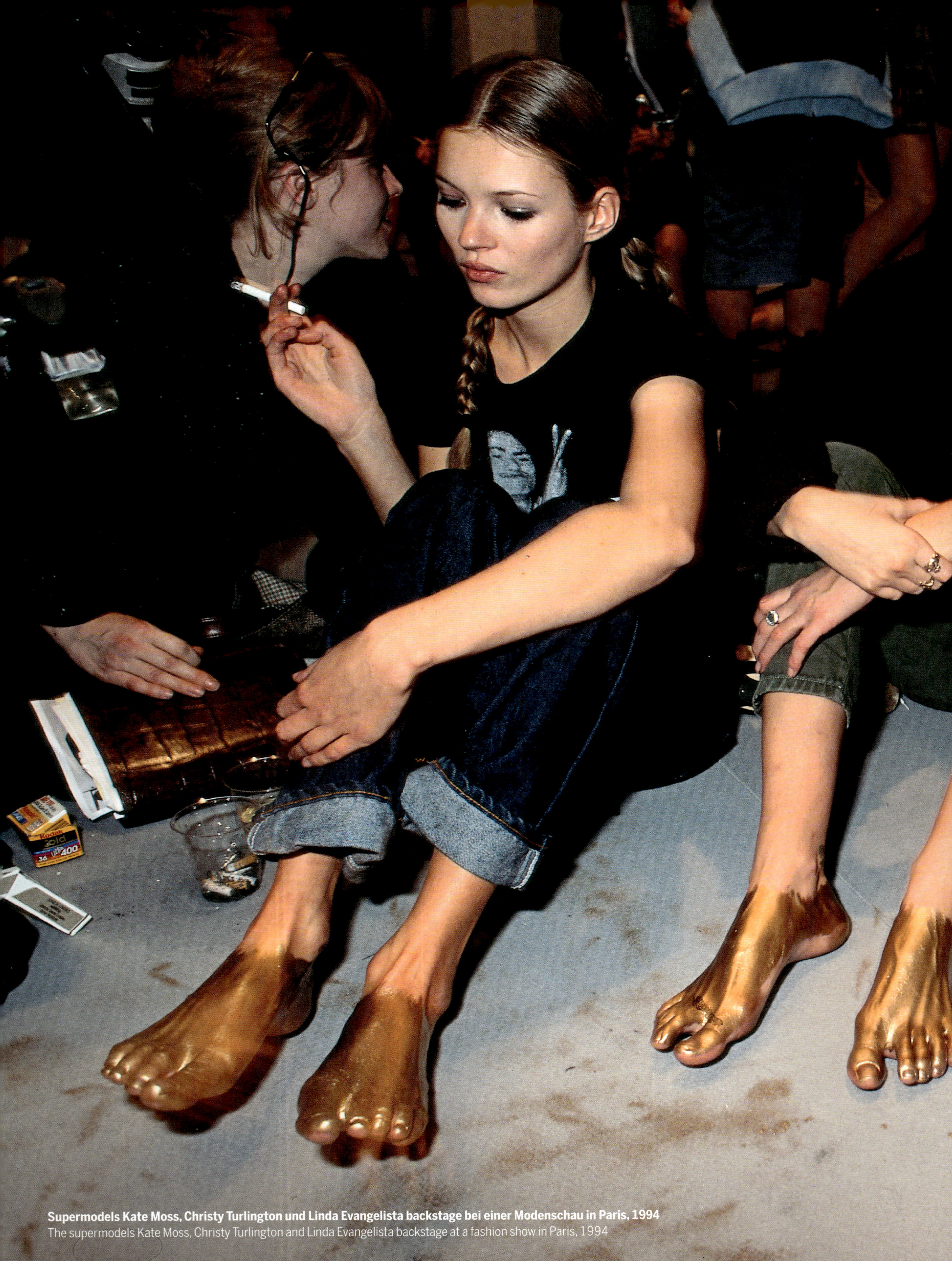

Supermodels Kate Moss, Christy Turlington und Linda Evangelista backstage bei einer Modenschau in Paris, 1994
The supermodels Kate Moss, Christy Turlington and Linda Evangelista backstage at a fashion show in Paris, 1994

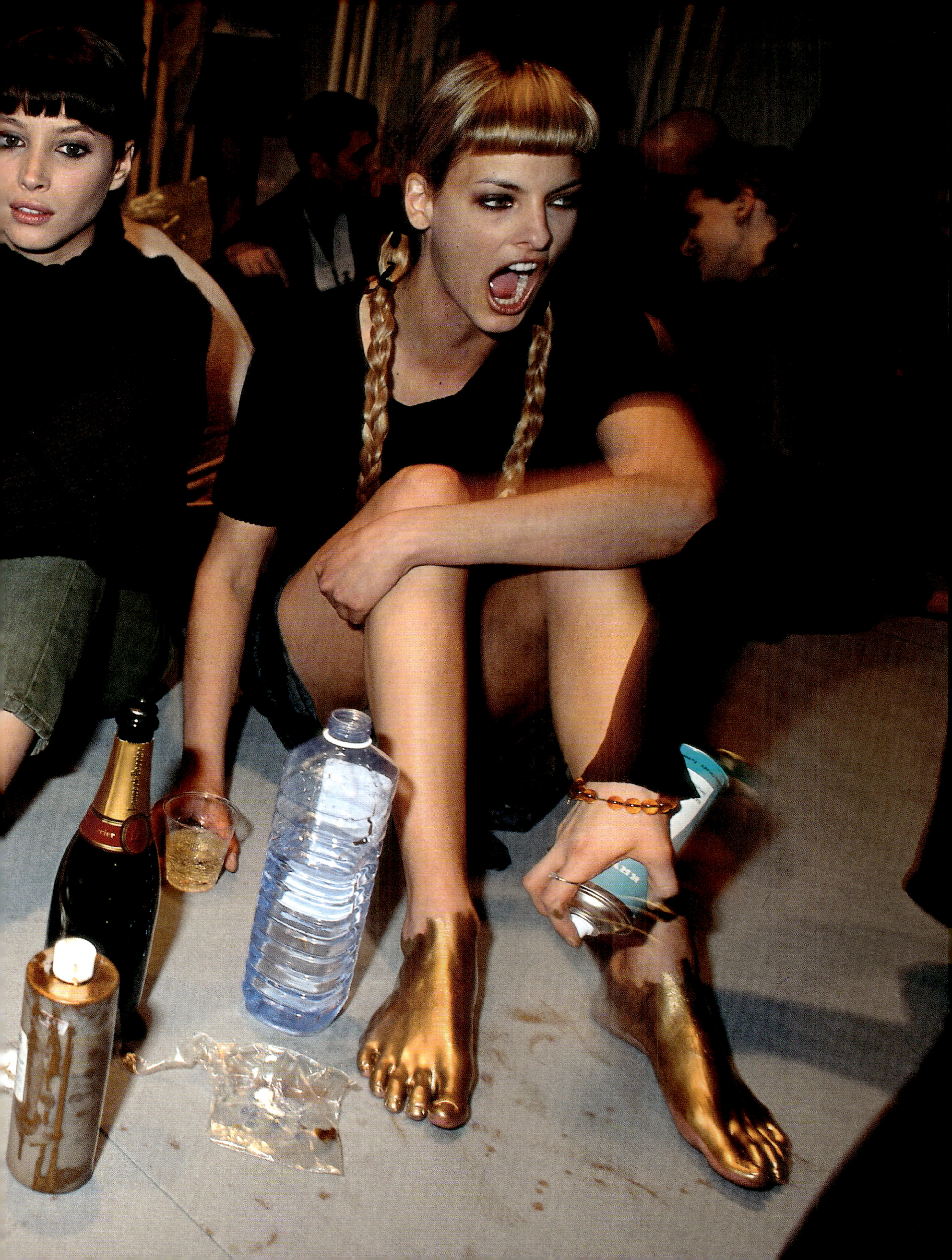

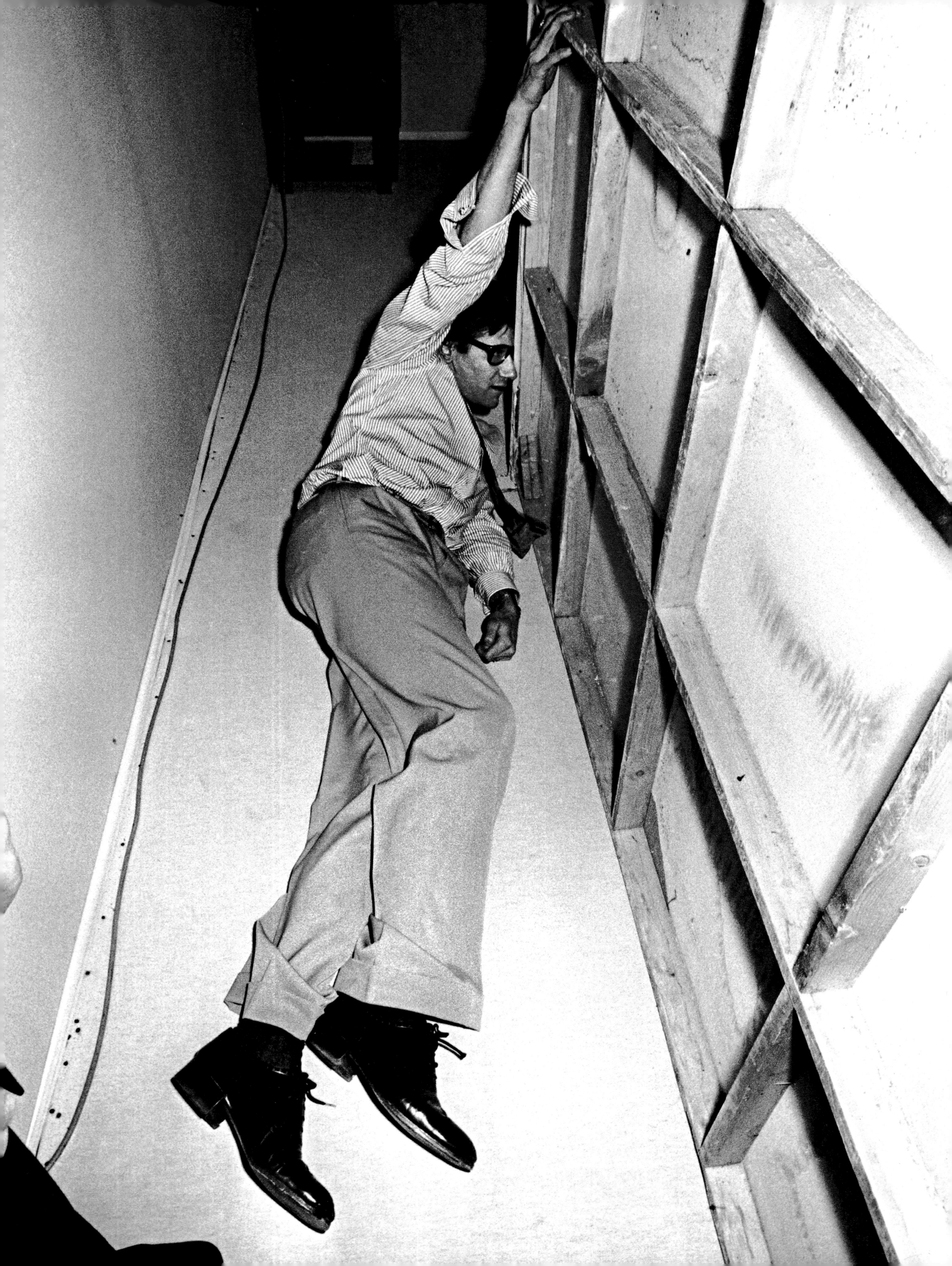

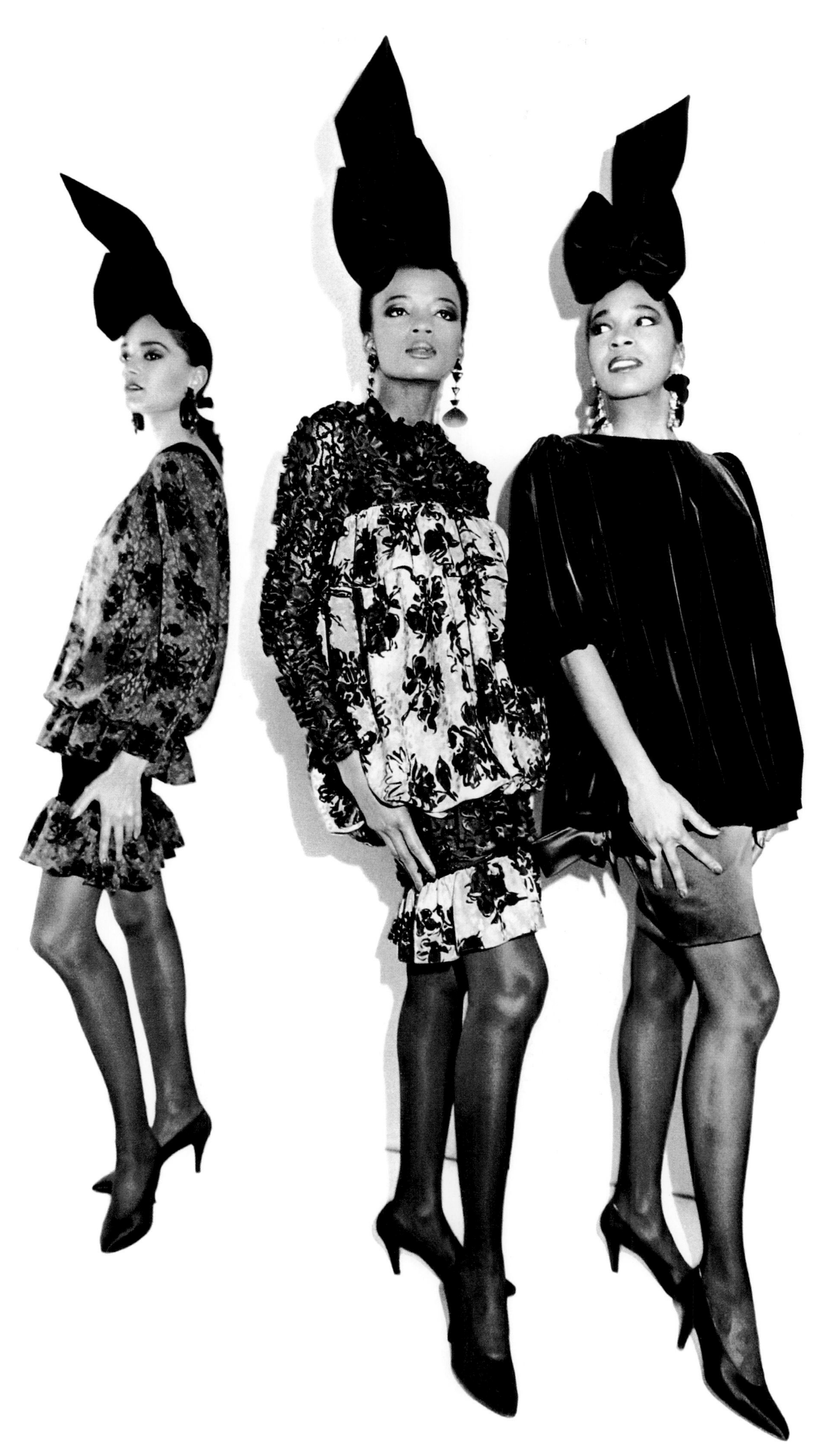

Designer Yves Saint Laurent, Paris, 1978
The designer Yves Saint Laurent, Paris, 1978

Mode, Paris, 1987
Fashion, Paris, 1987

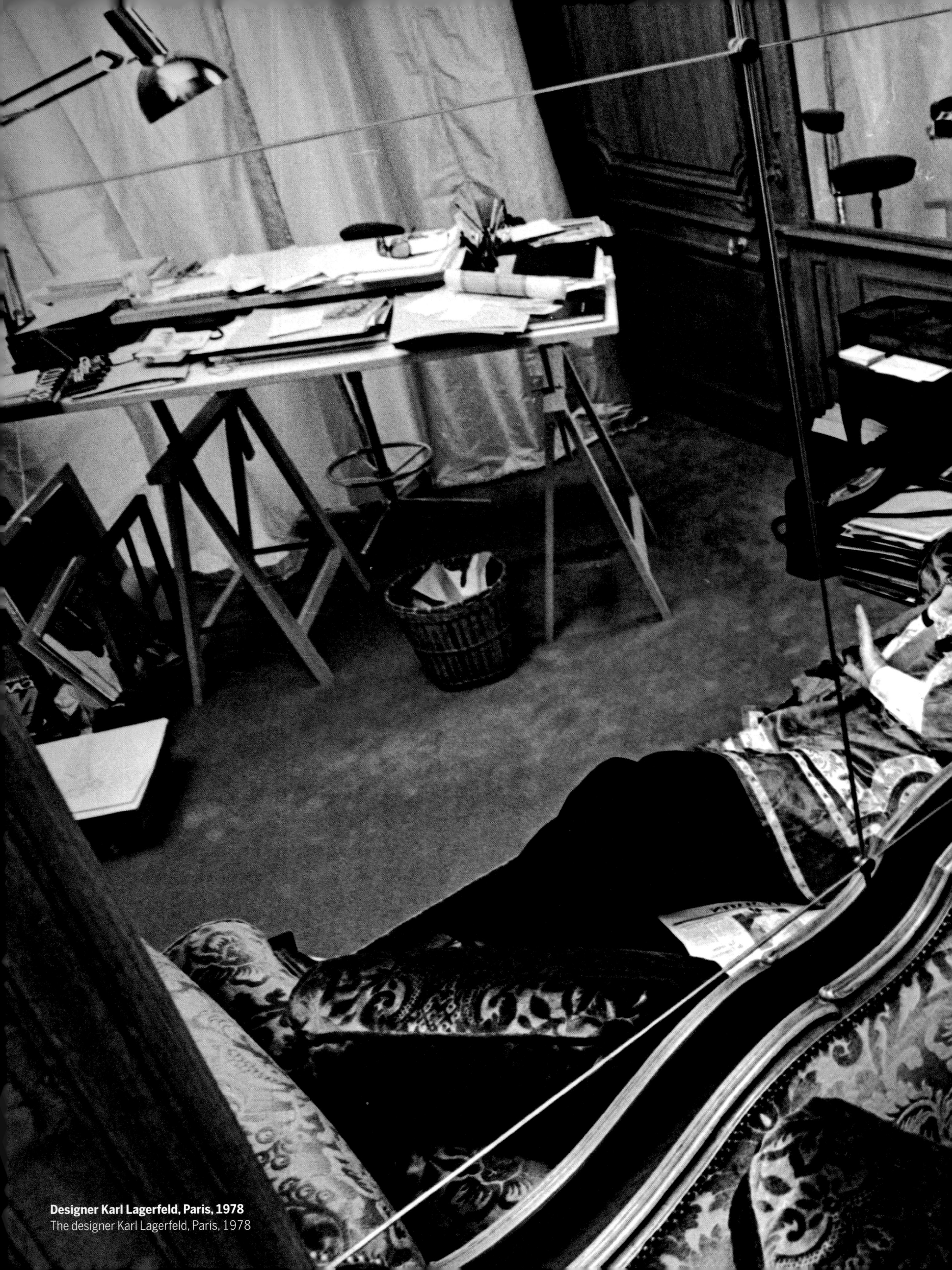

Designer Karl Lagerfeld, Paris, 1978
The designer Karl Lagerfeld, Paris, 1978

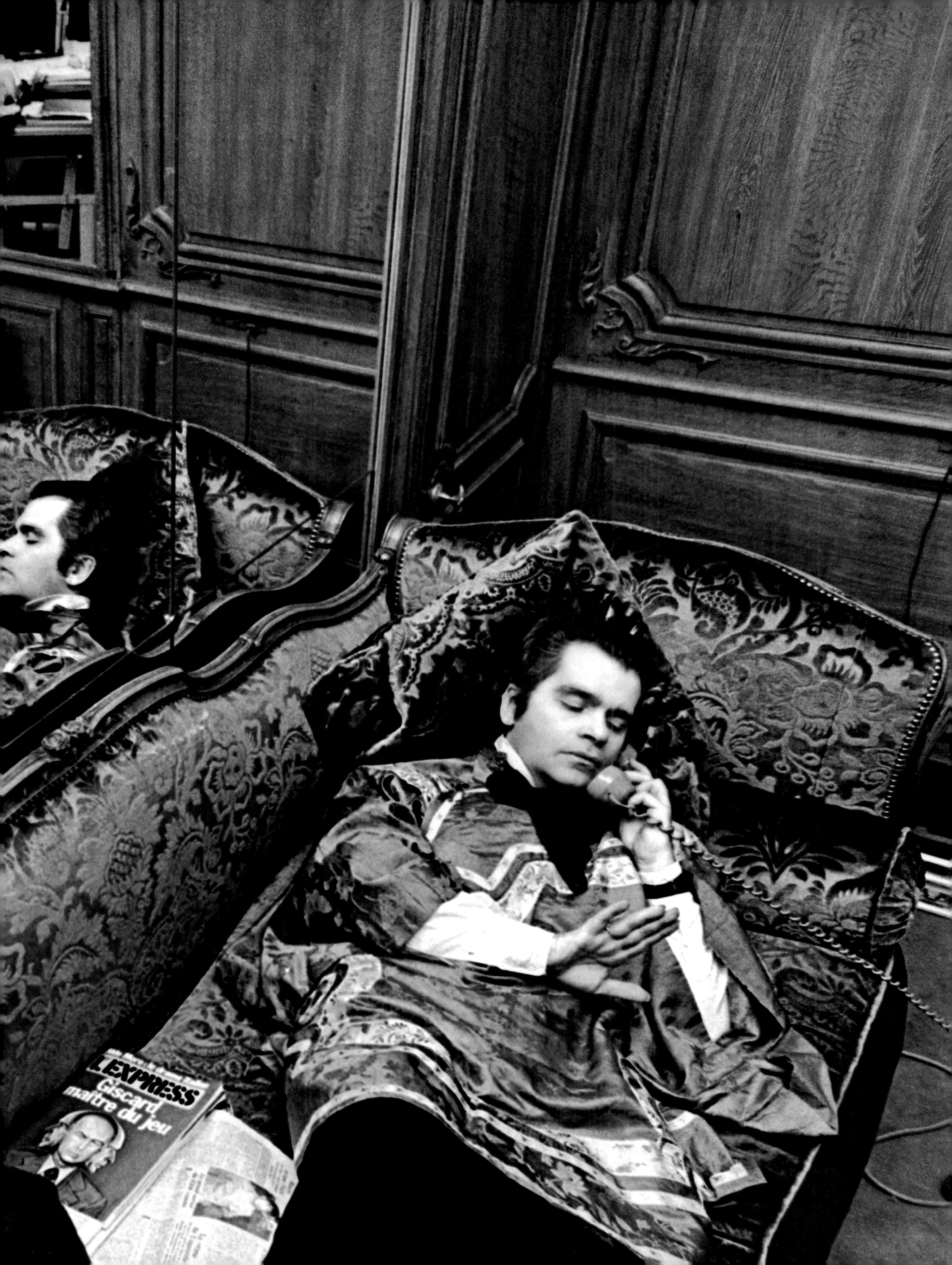
L'EXPRESS
Giscard
maître du jeu

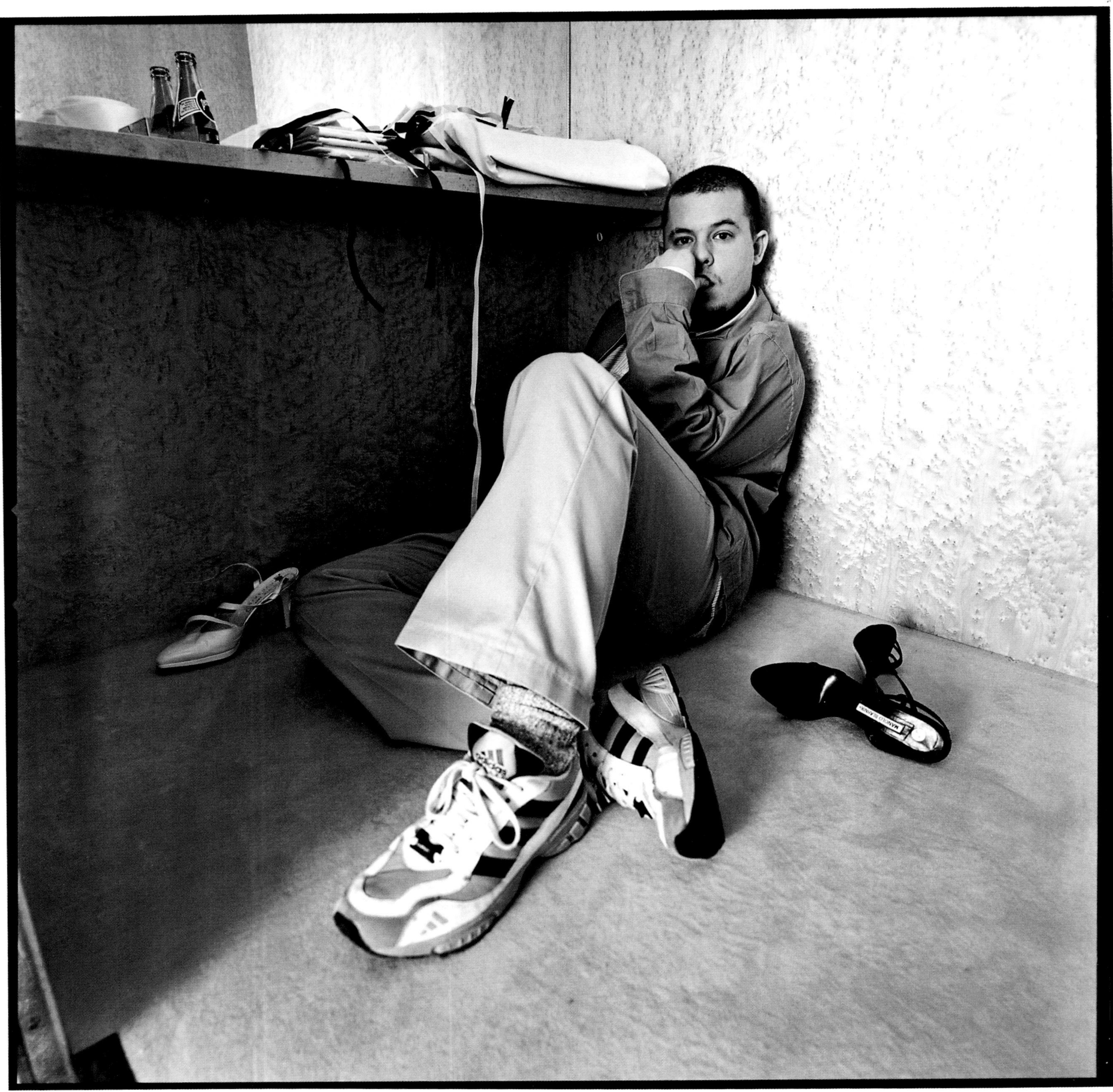

Designer Alexander McQueen, Paris, 1996
The designer Alexander McQueen, Paris, 1996

Designer Yohji Yamamoto, Paris, 1987
The designer Yohji Yamamoto, Paris, 1987

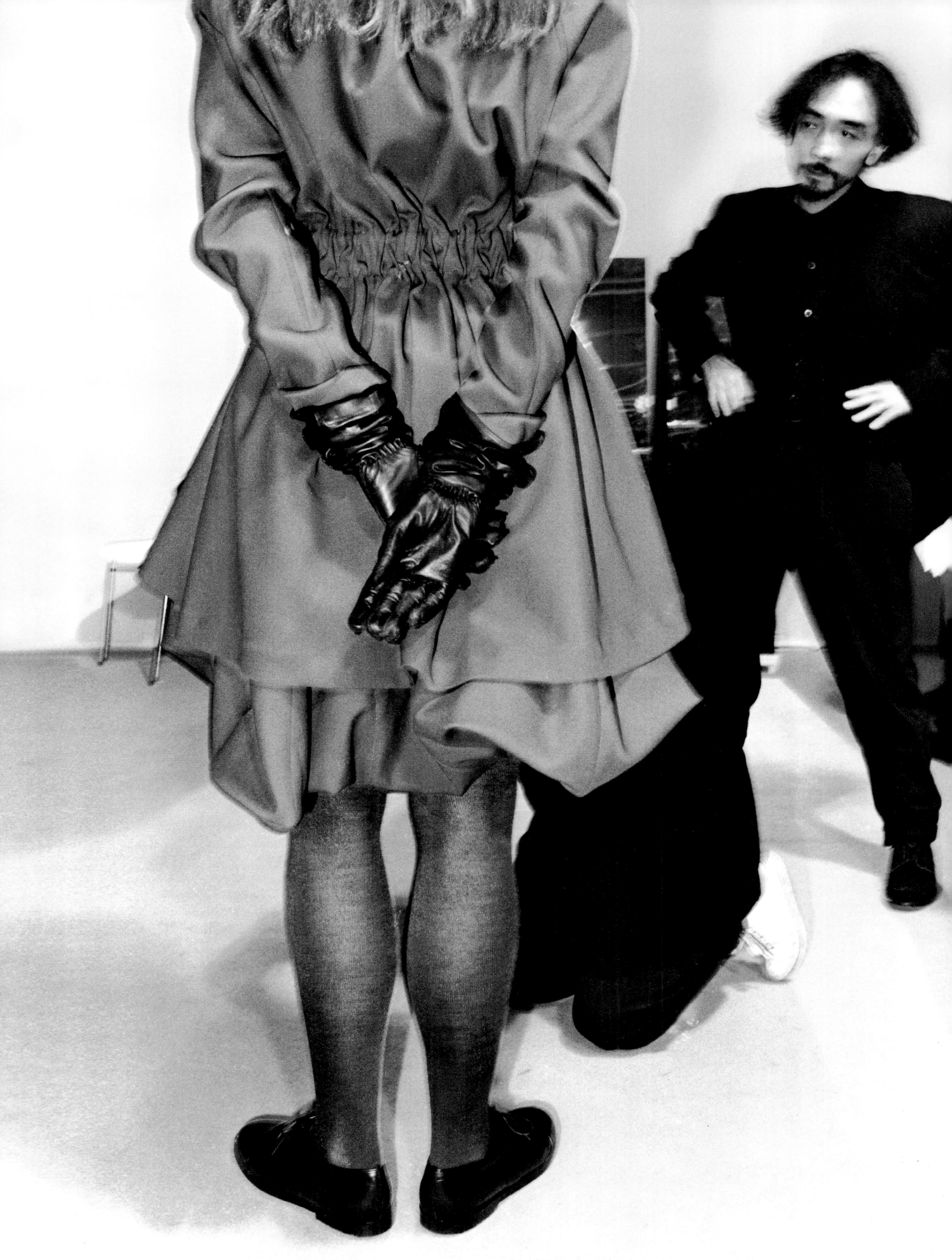

Mann mit Pin-up-Kalender, Detroit, USA, 1982
A man with a pin-up calendar, Detroit, USA, 1982

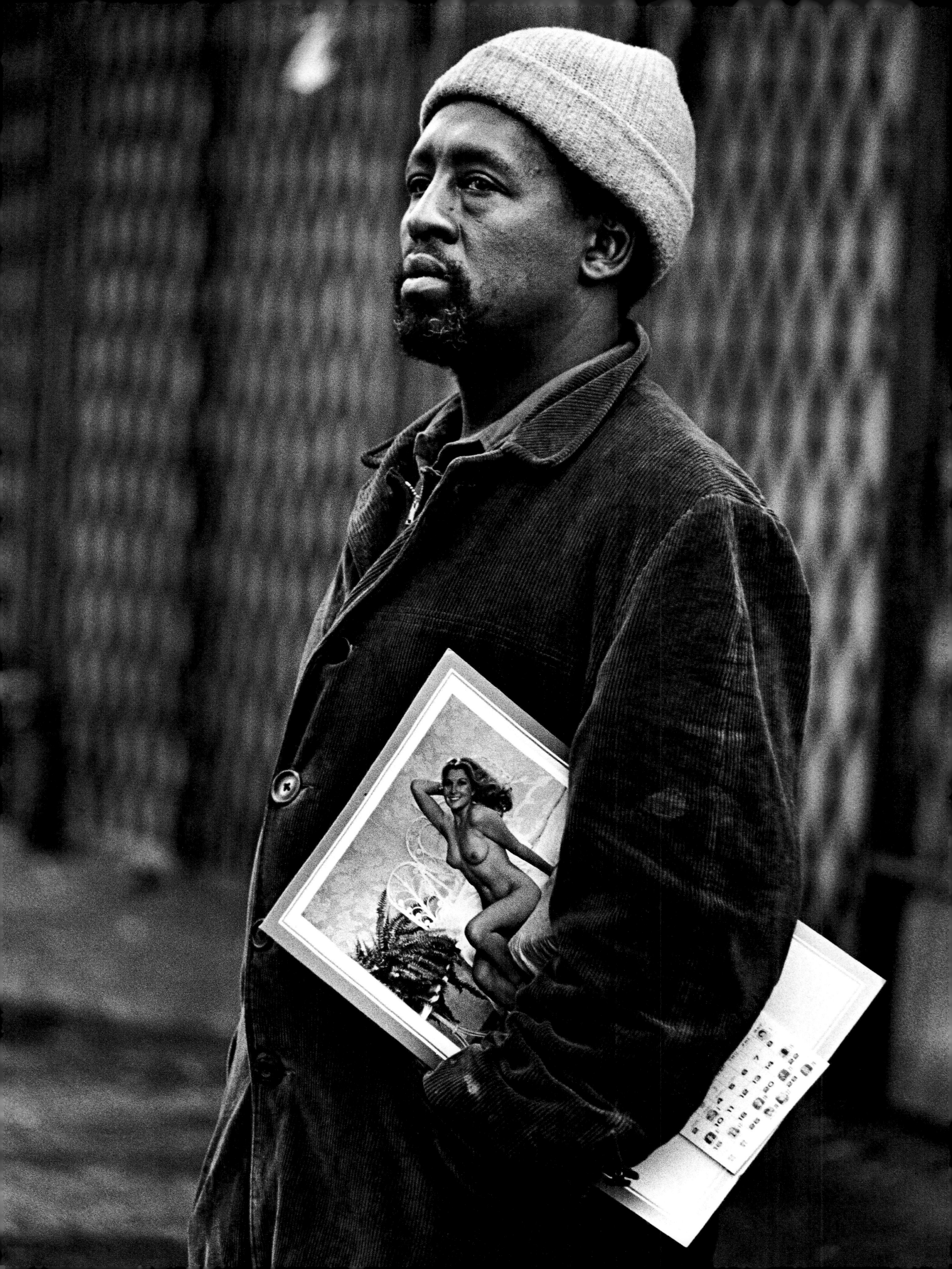

Muhammad Ali, Santa Monica, Kalifornien, USA, 1984
Muhammad Ali, Santa Monica, California, USA, 1984

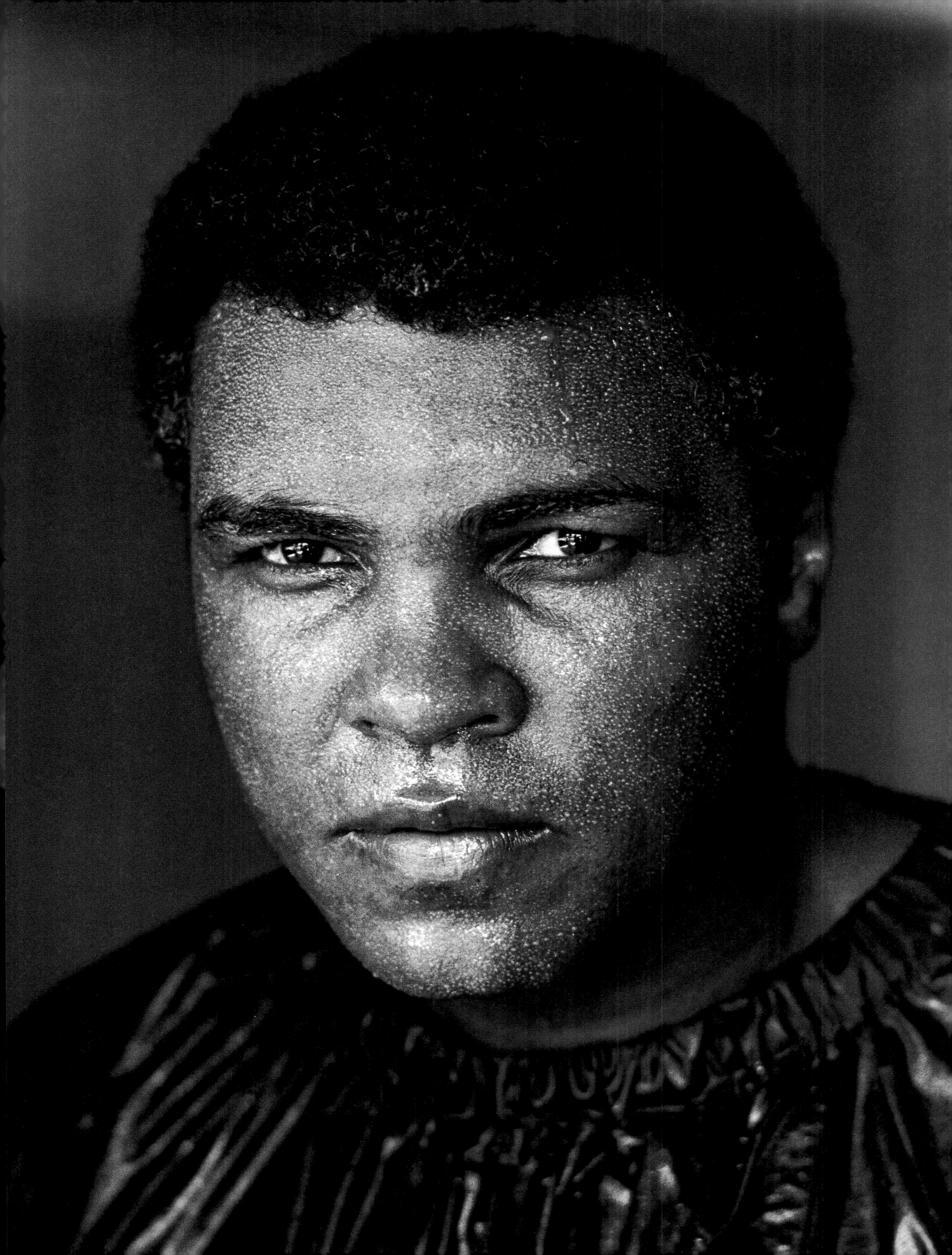

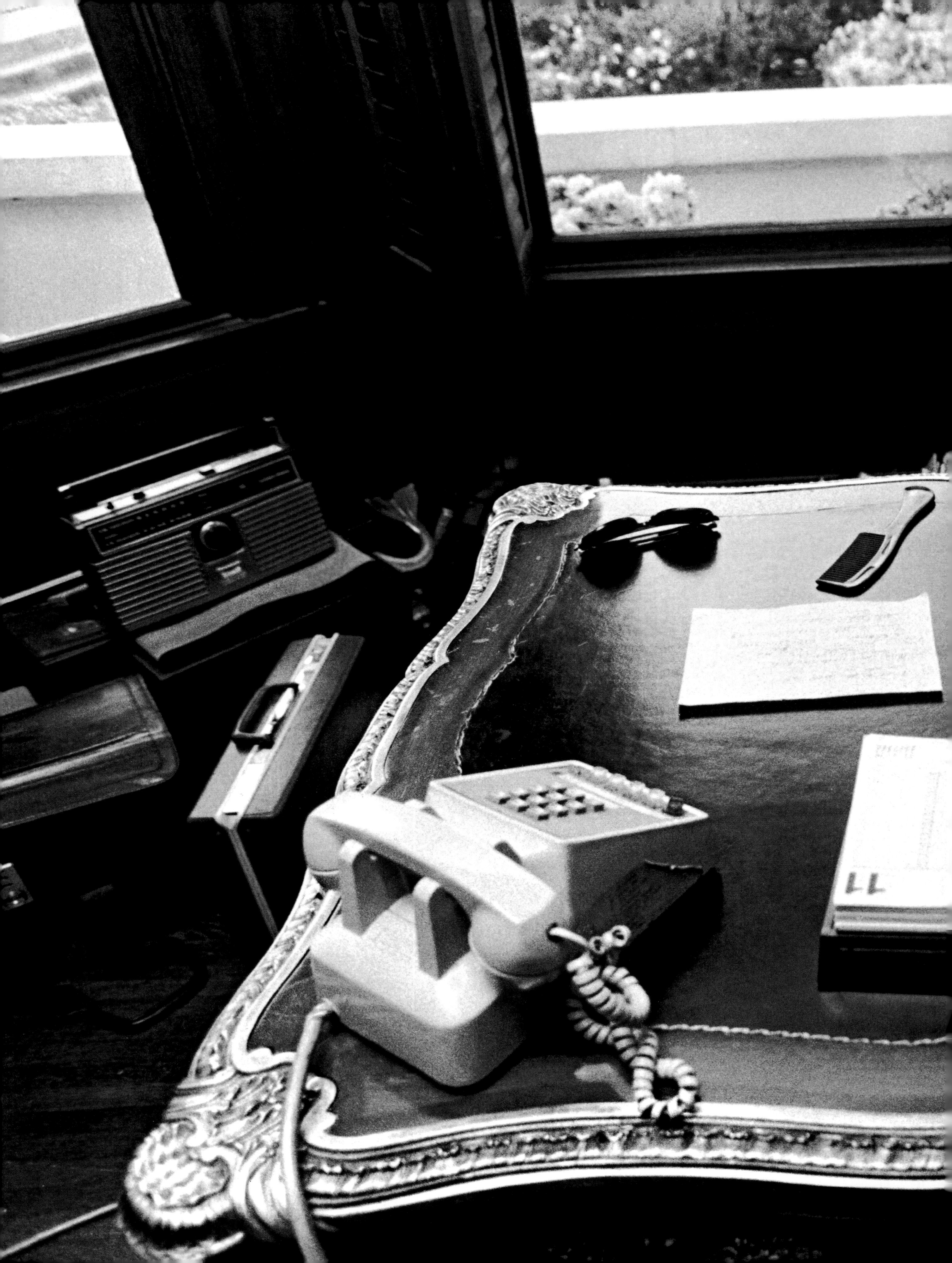

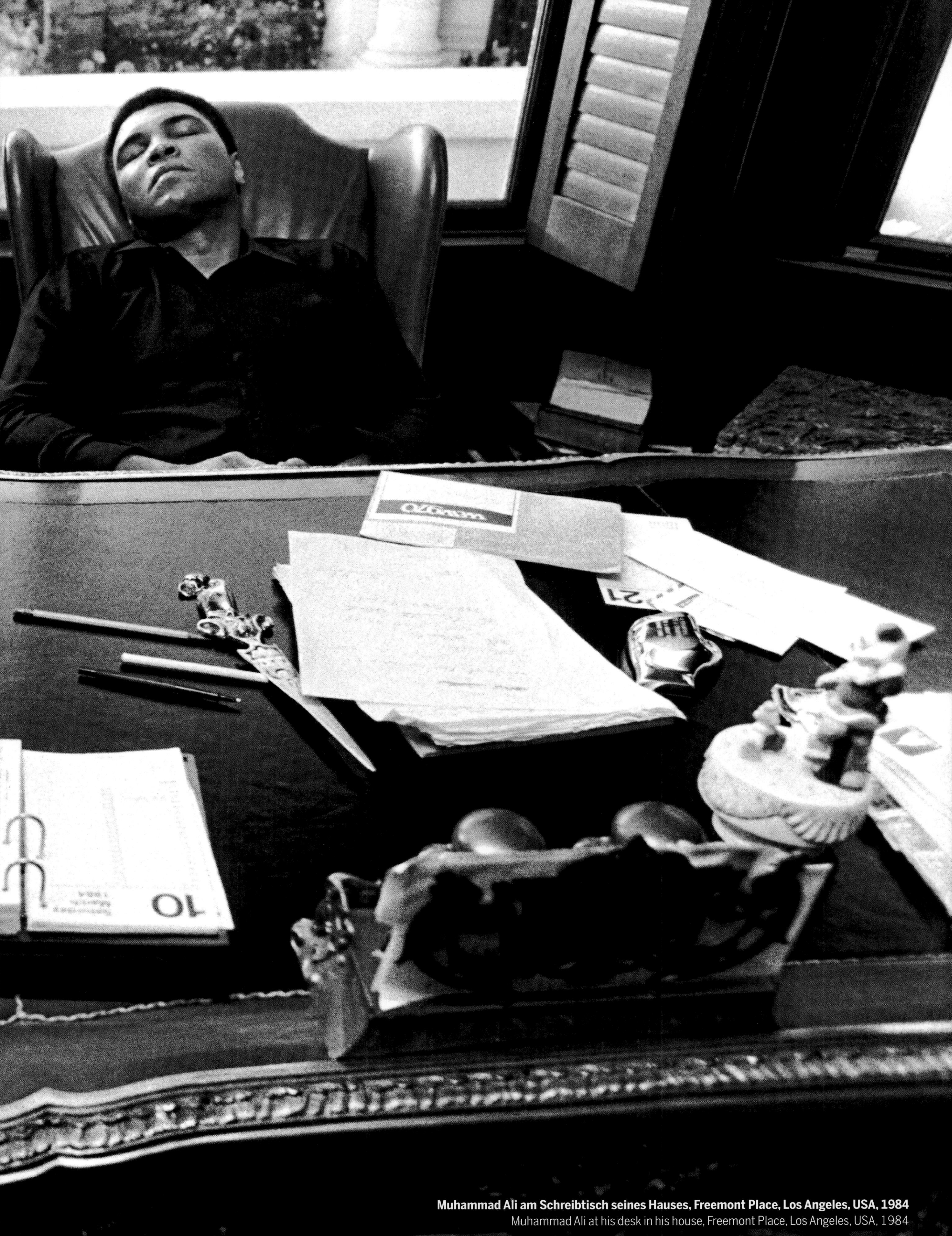

Muhammad Ali am Schreibtisch seines Hauses, Freemont Place, Los Angeles, USA, 1984
Muhammad Ali at his desk in his house, Freemont Place, Los Angeles, USA, 1984

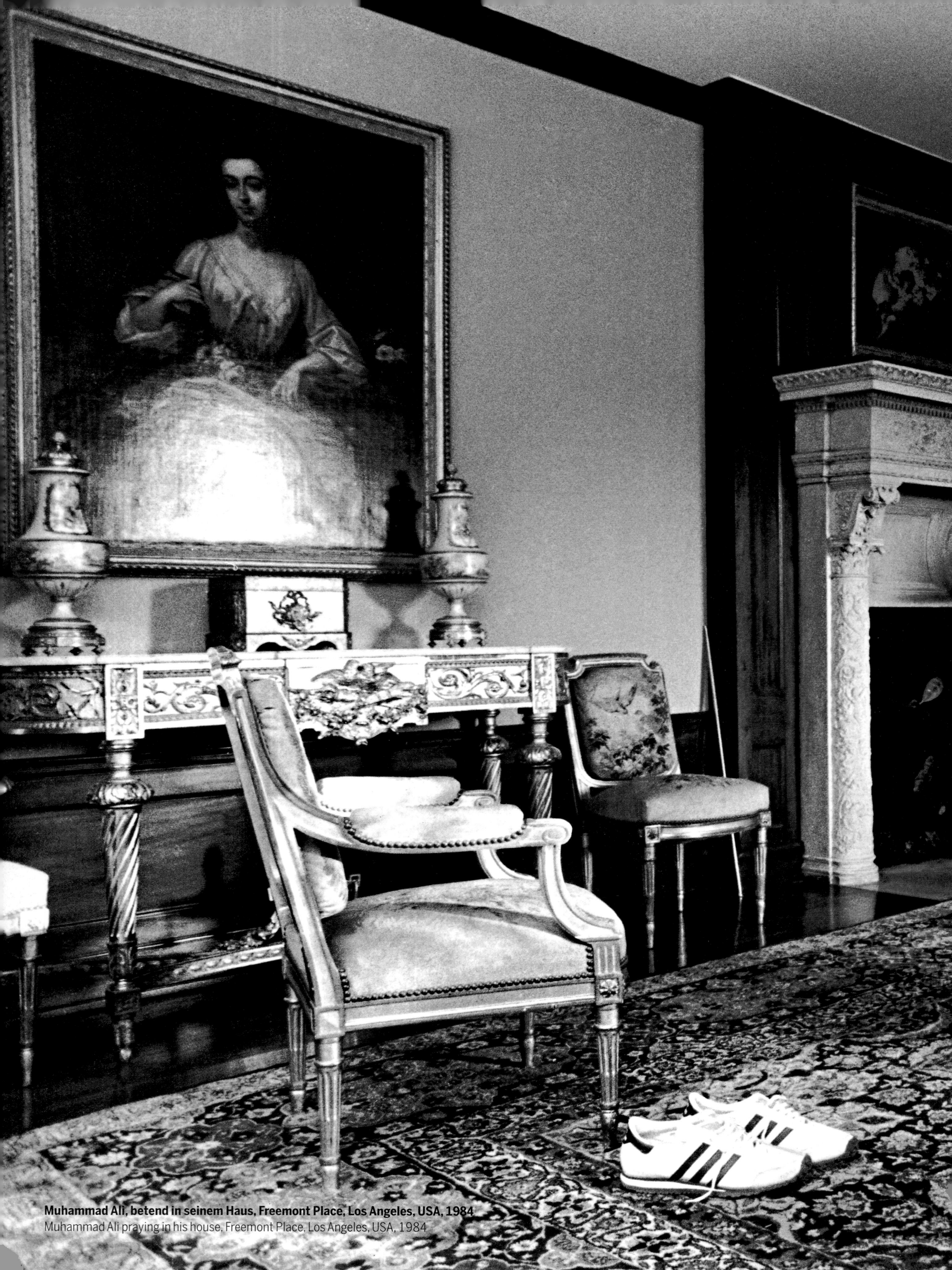

Muhammad Ali, betend in seinem Haus, Freemont Place, Los Angeles, USA, 1984
Muhammad Ali praying in his house, Freemont Place, Los Angeles, USA, 1984

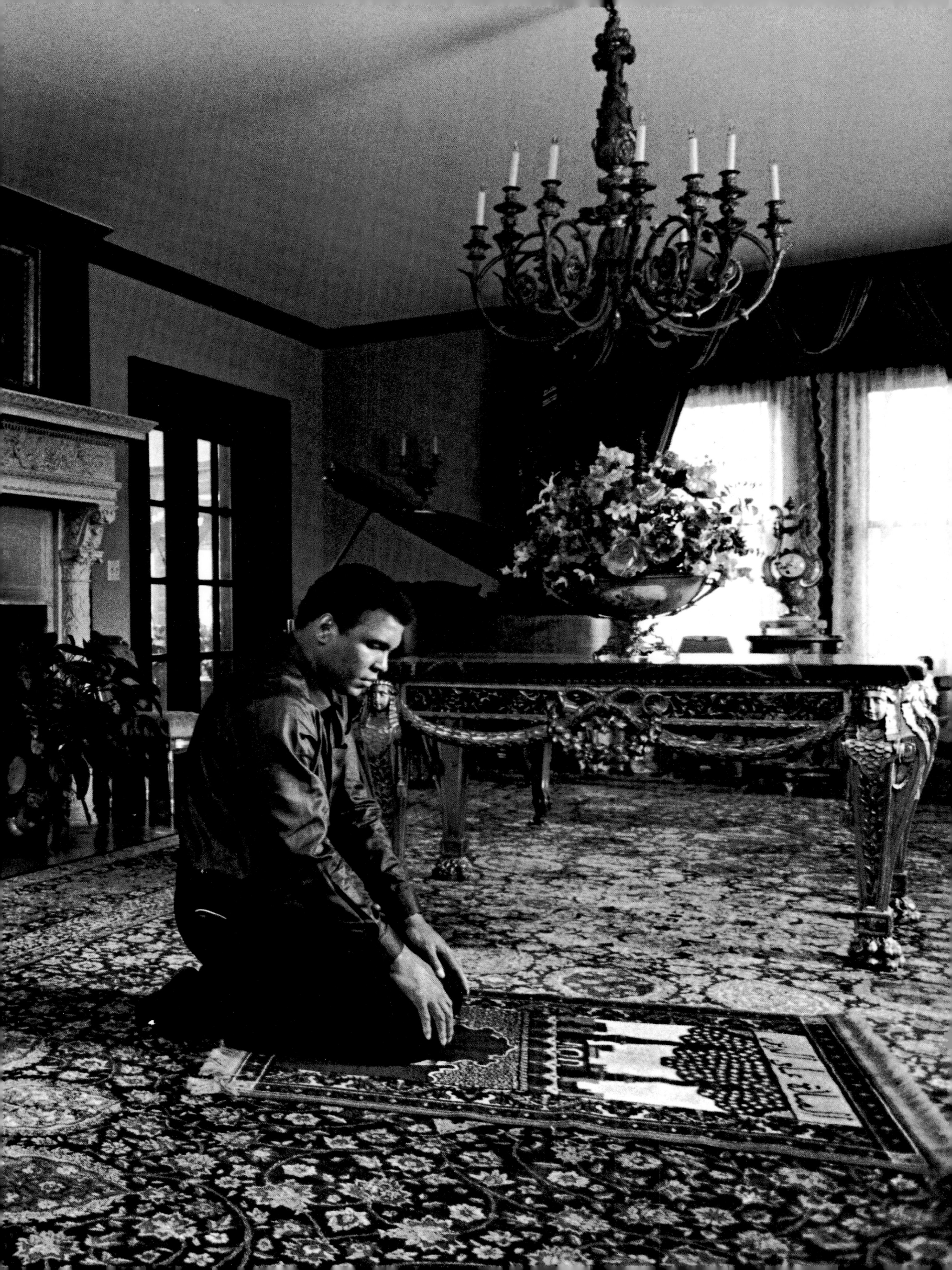

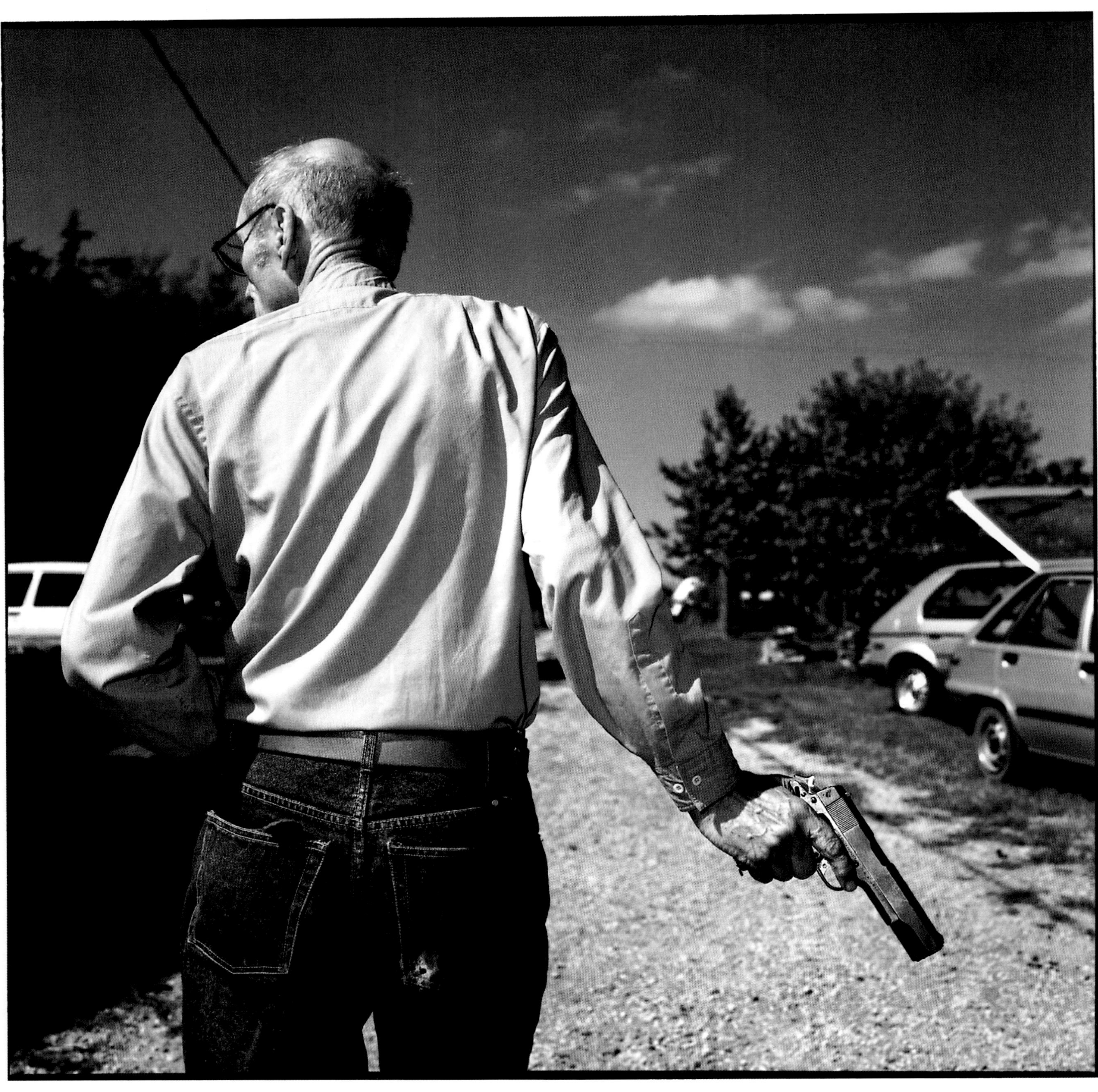

Schriftsteller William S. Burroughs, Lawrence, Kansas, USA, 1987
The writer William S. Burroughs, Lawrence, Kansas, USA, 1987

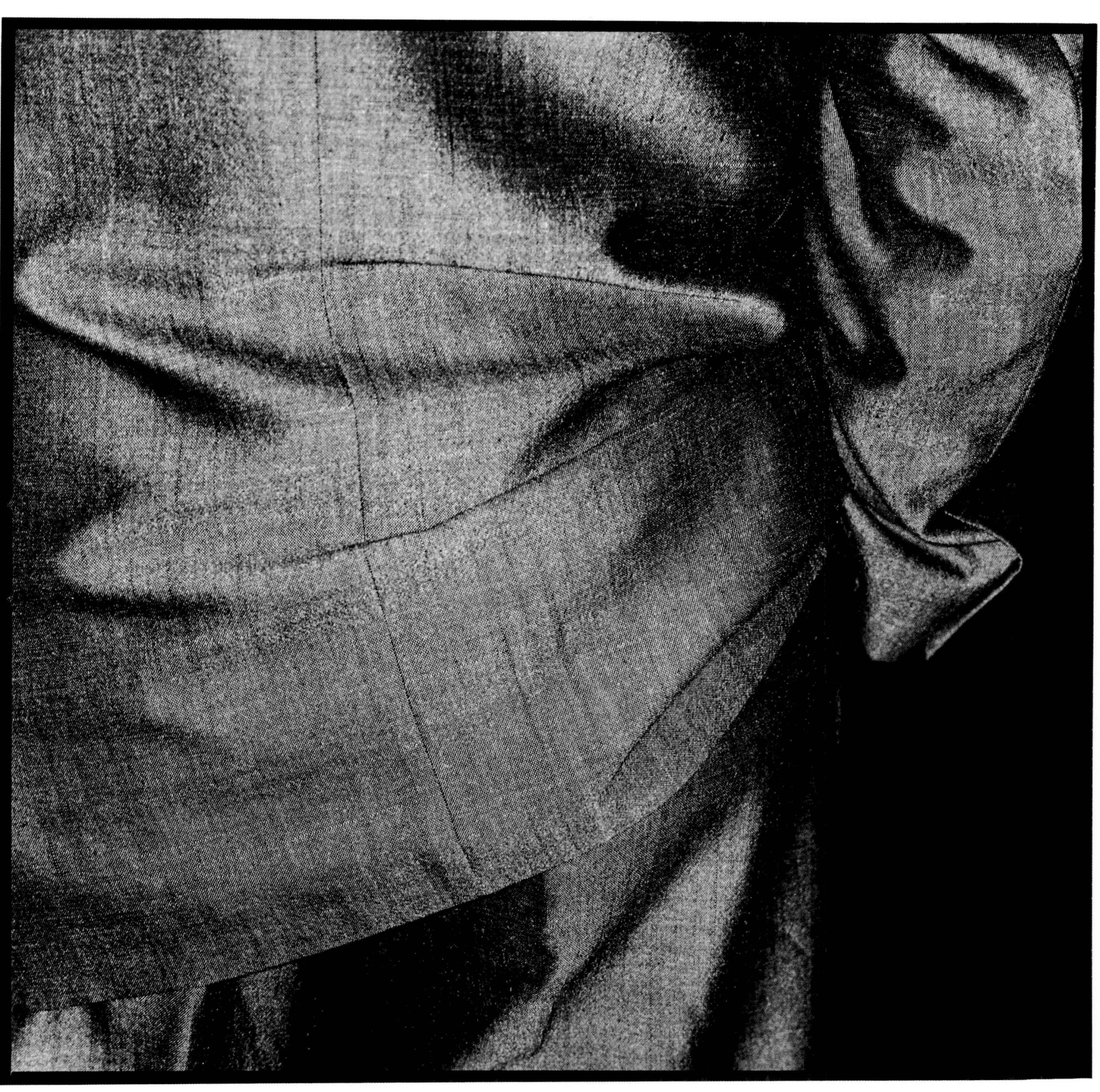

Autor und Journalist Gay Talese, New York, USA, 1998
The writer and journalist Gay Talese, New York, USA, 1998

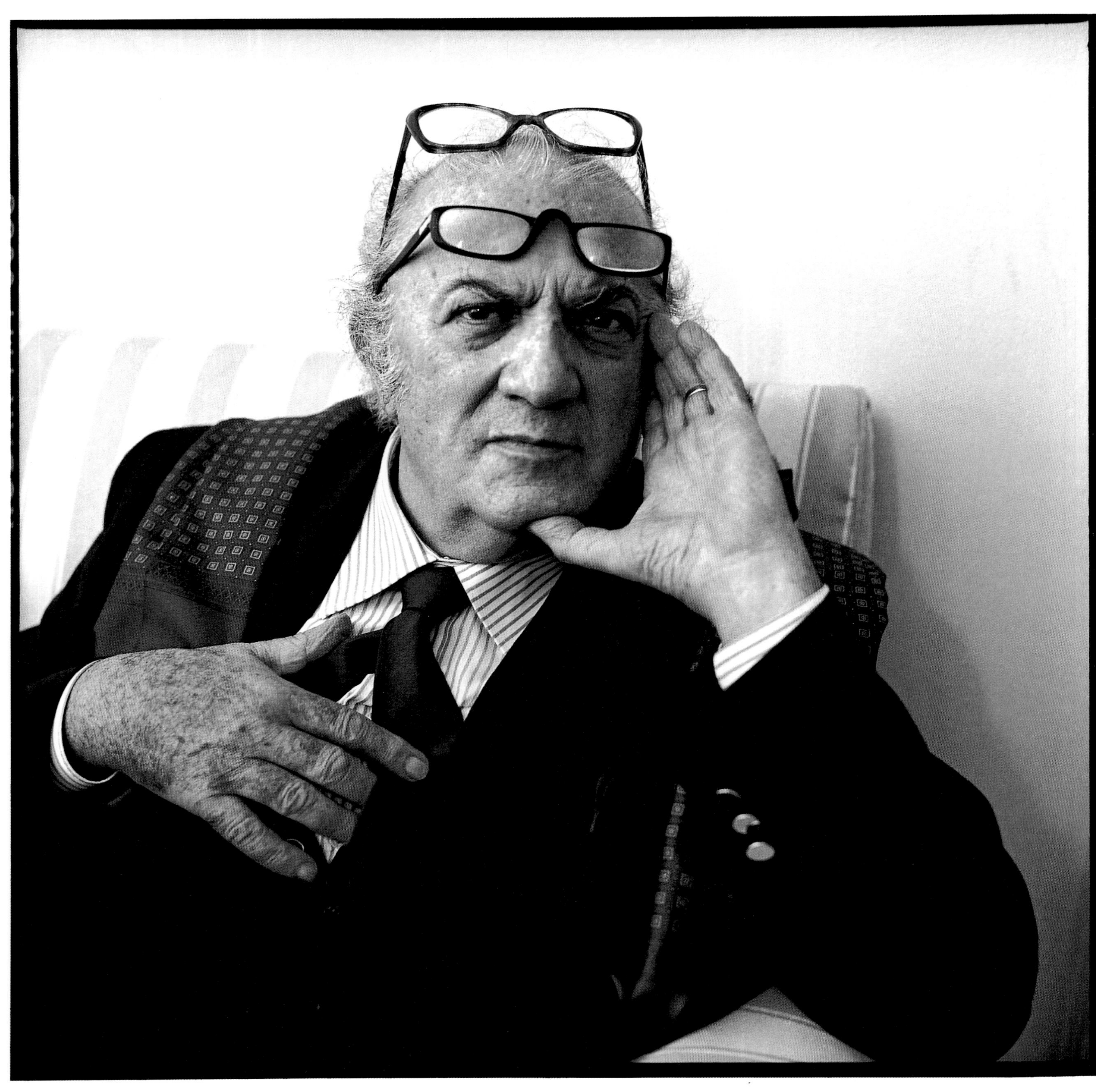

Regisseur Federico Fellini, Rom, 1987
The director Federico Fellini, Rome, 1987

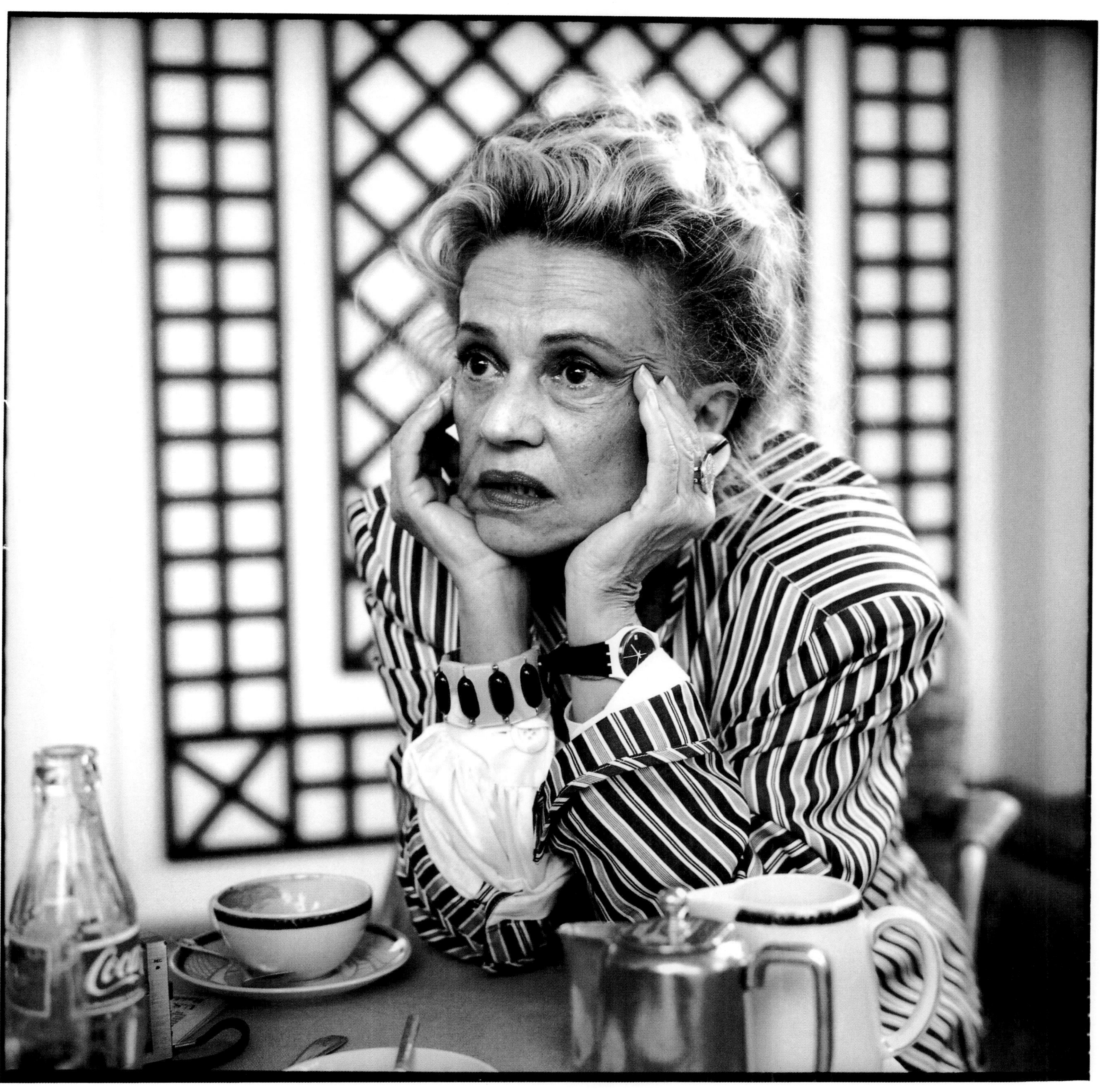

Schauspielerin Jeanne Moreau, Zürich, 1987
The actress Jeanne Moreau, Zurich, 1987

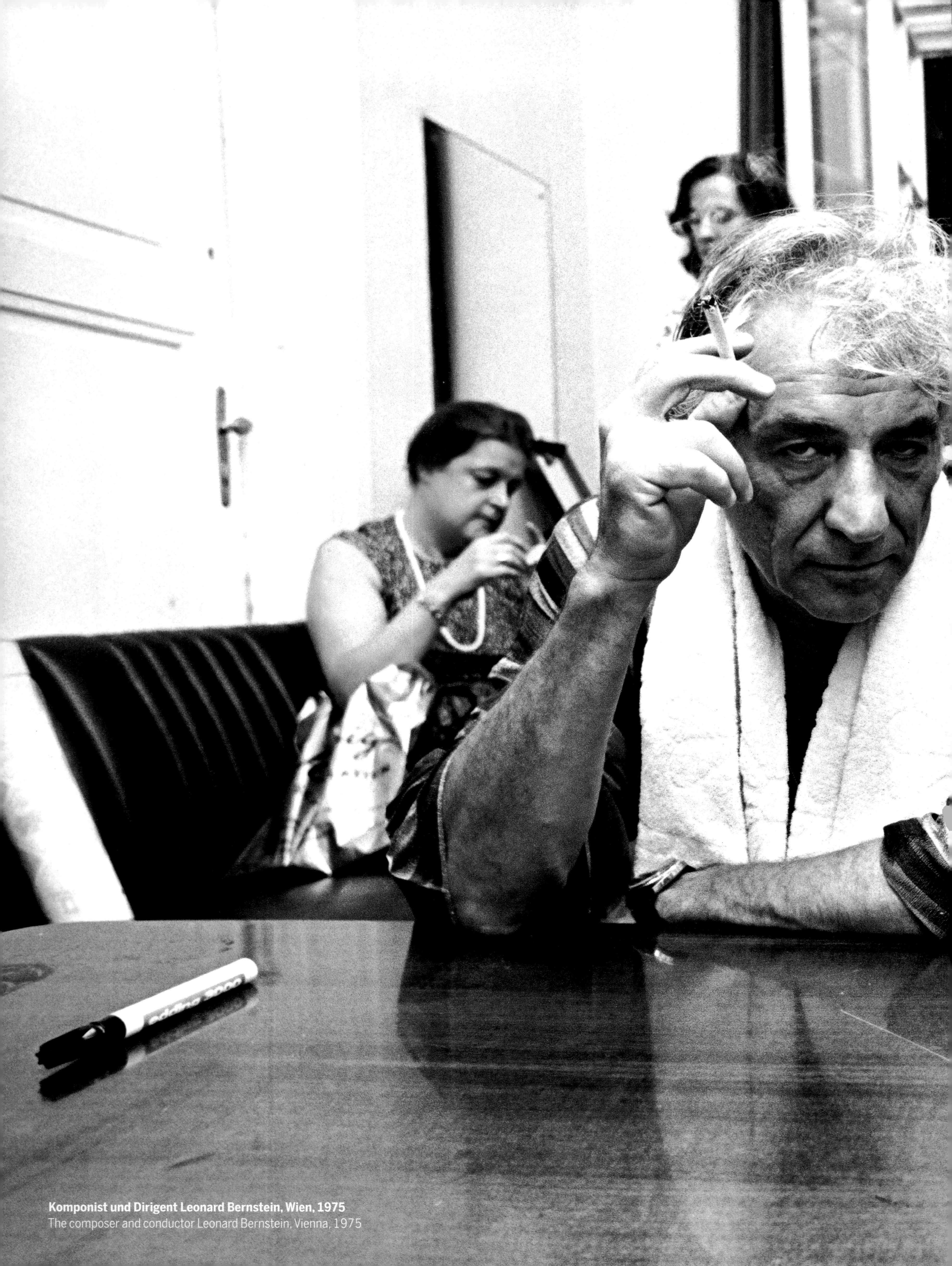

Komponist und Dirigent Leonard Bernstein, Wien, 1975
The composer and conductor Leonard Bernstein, Vienna, 1975

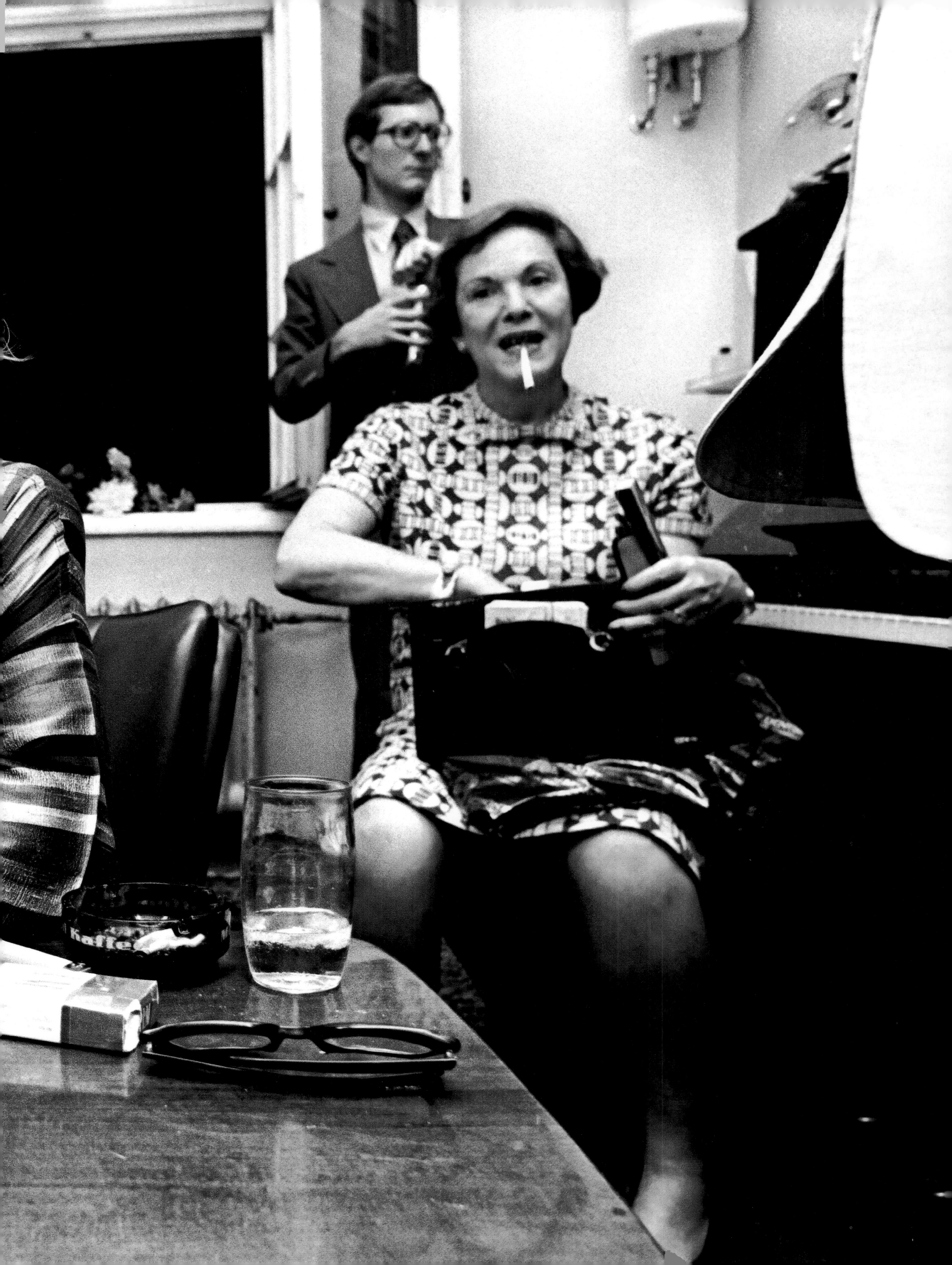

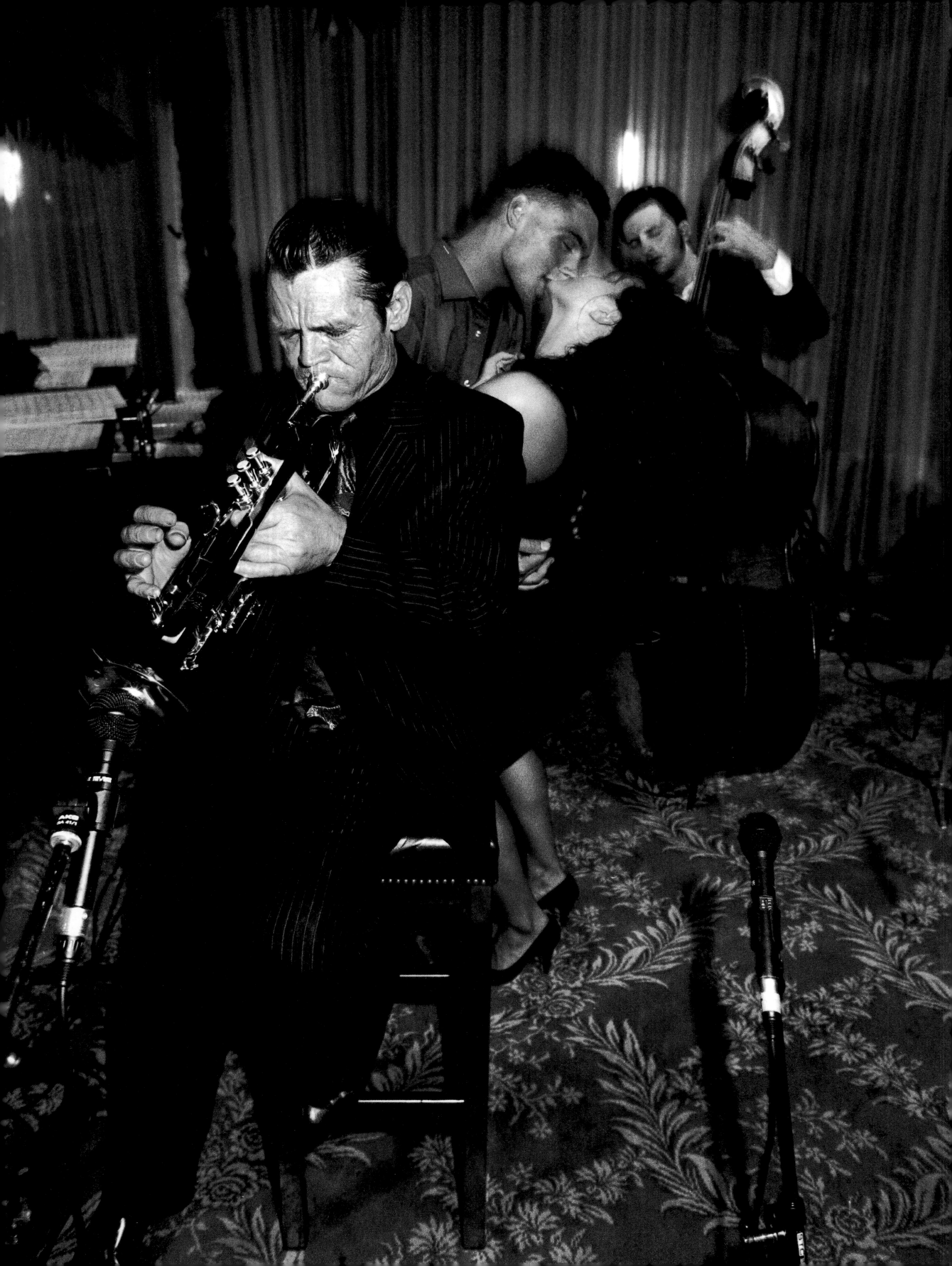

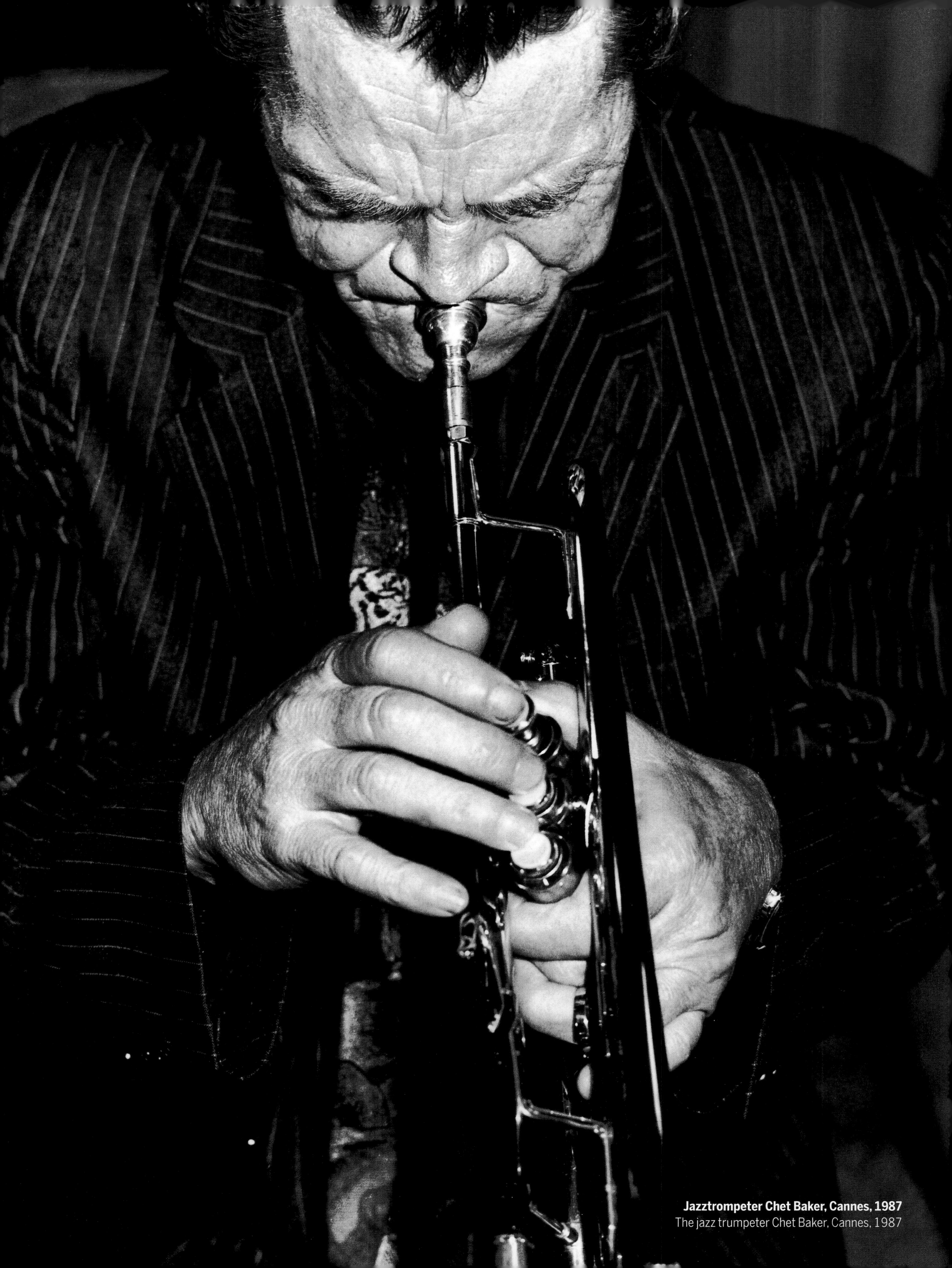

Jazztrompeter Chet Baker, Cannes, 1987
The jazz trumpeter Chet Baker, Cannes, 1987

Sängerin und Schauspielerin Madonna, New York, USA, 1983
The singer and actress Madonna, New York, USA, 1983

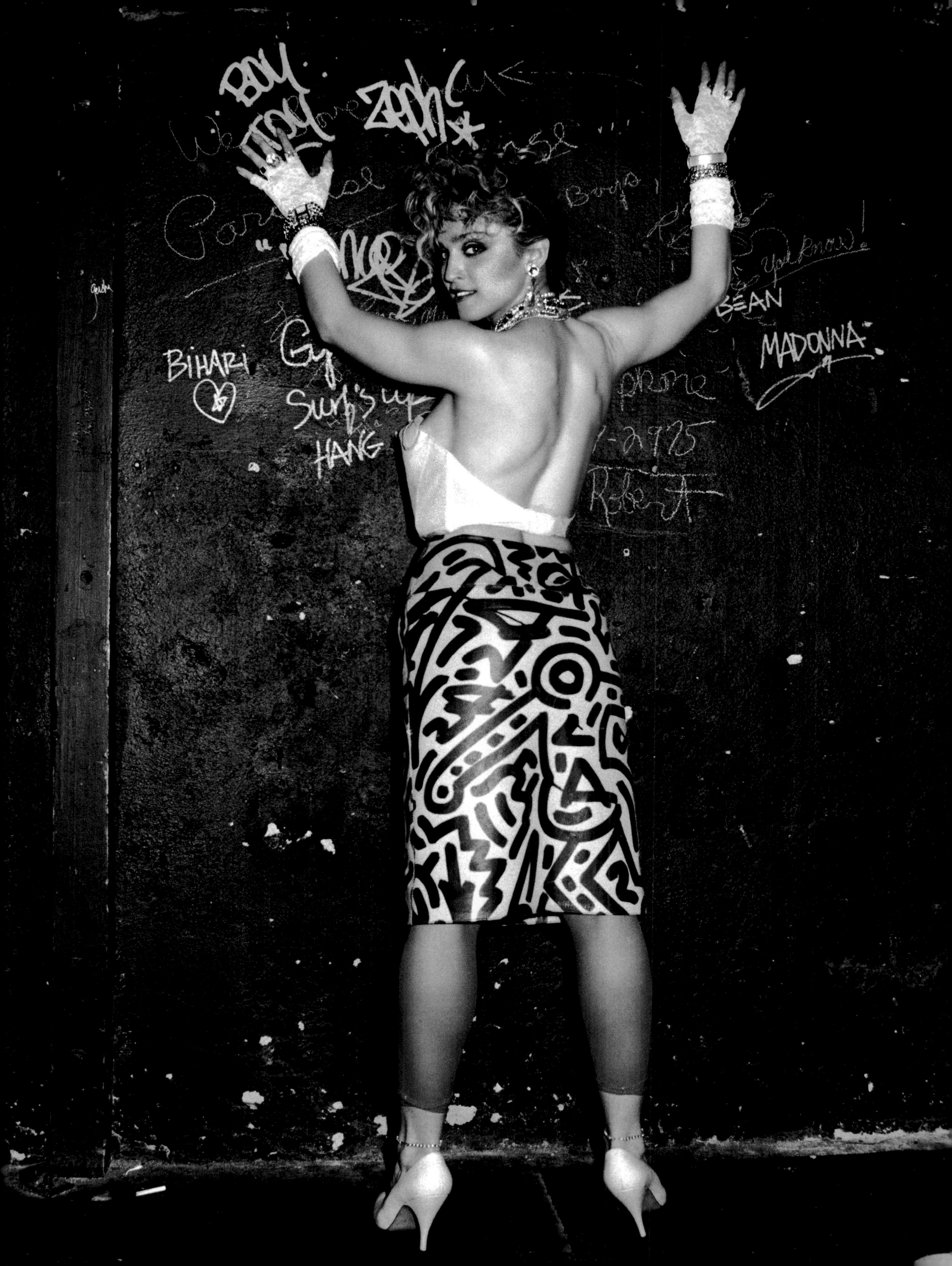

BOY
ZEPHU
Bihari Gy
Surf's up
HANG
BEAN
MADONNA
Robert

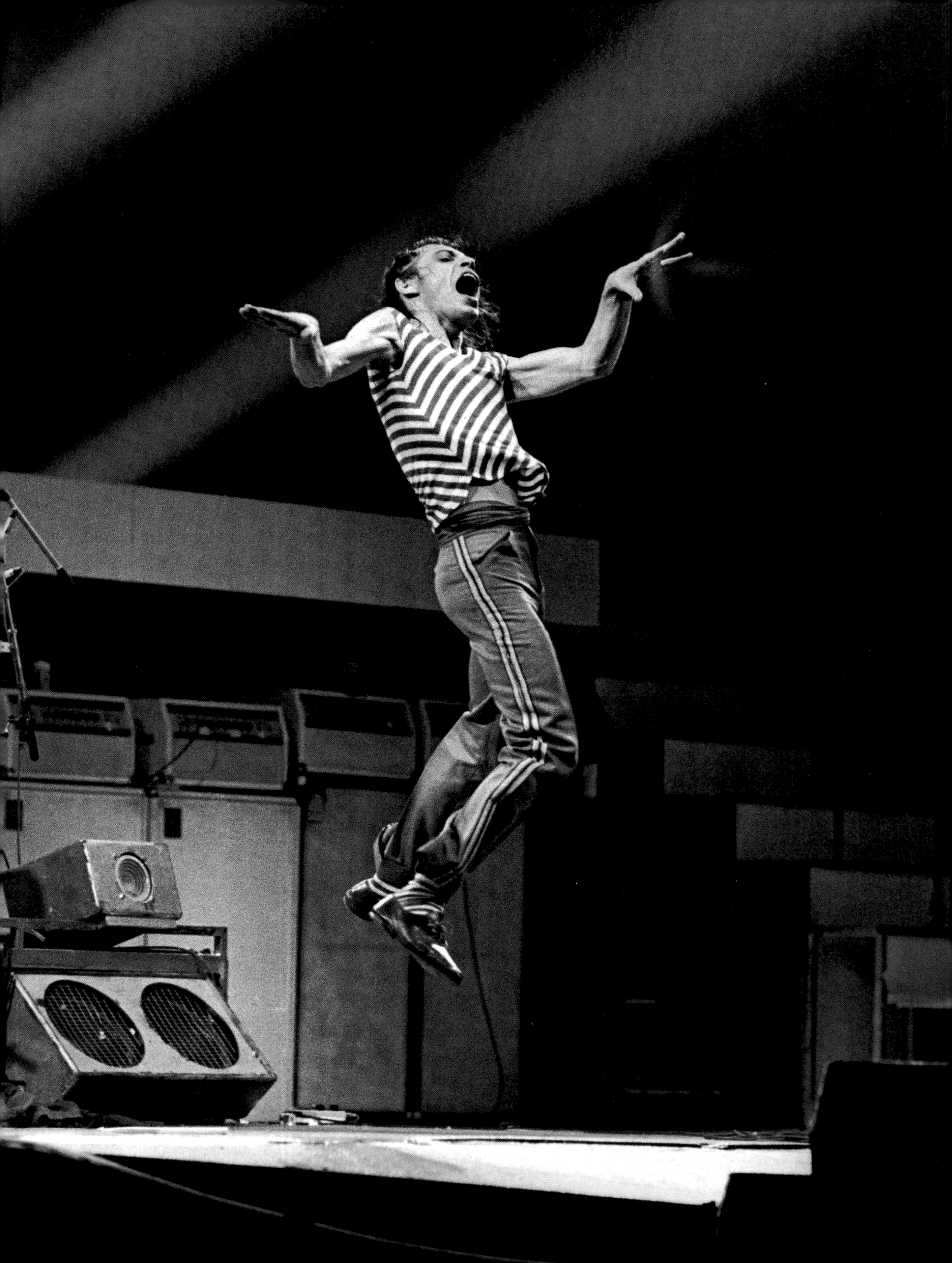

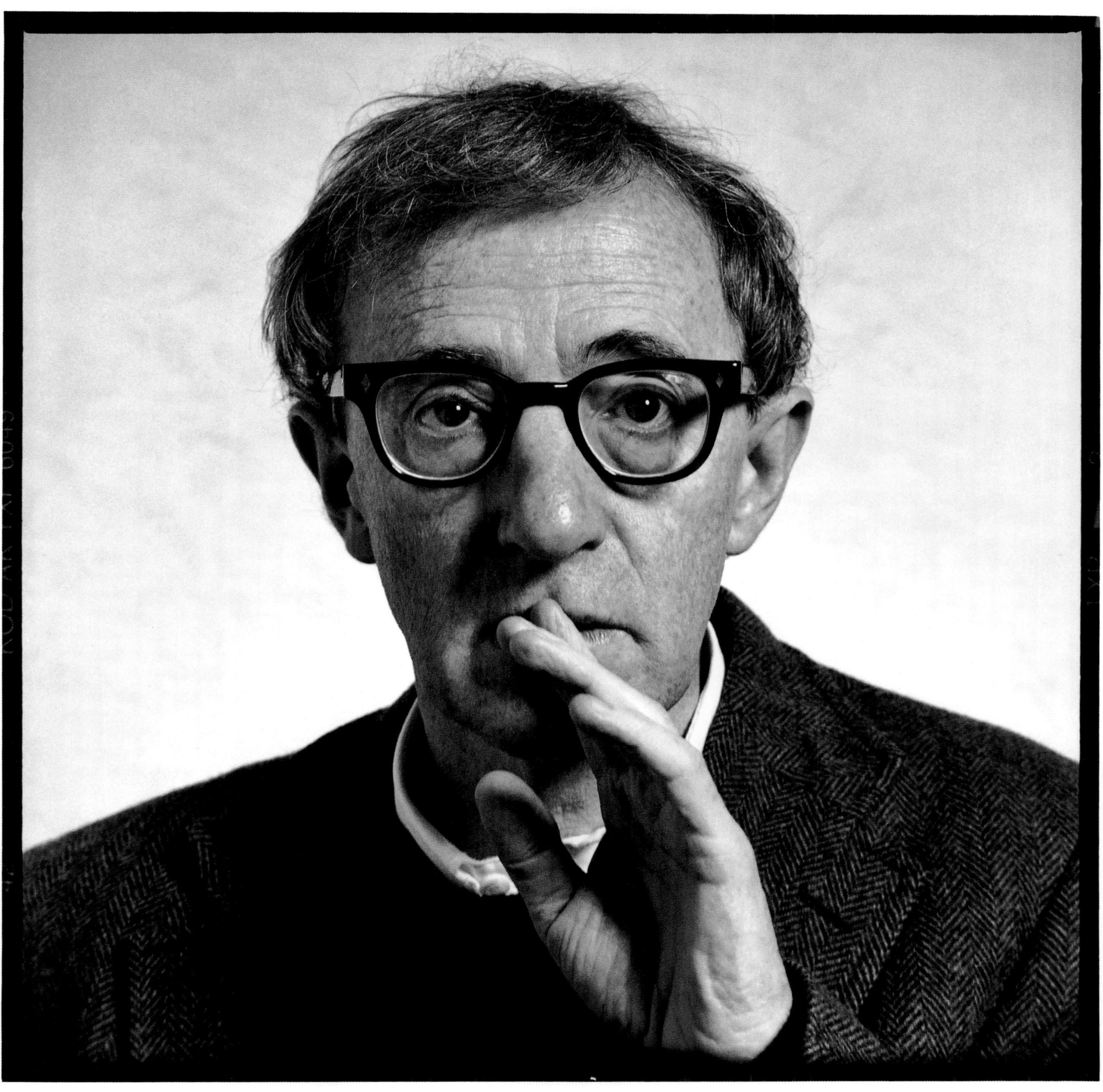

Schauspieler und Regisseur Woody Allen, Hamburg, 1994
The actor and director Woody Allen, Hamburg, 1994

Sänger der Rolling Stones, Mick Jagger, Köln, 1976
The Rolling Stones lead singer, Mick Jagger, Cologne, 1976

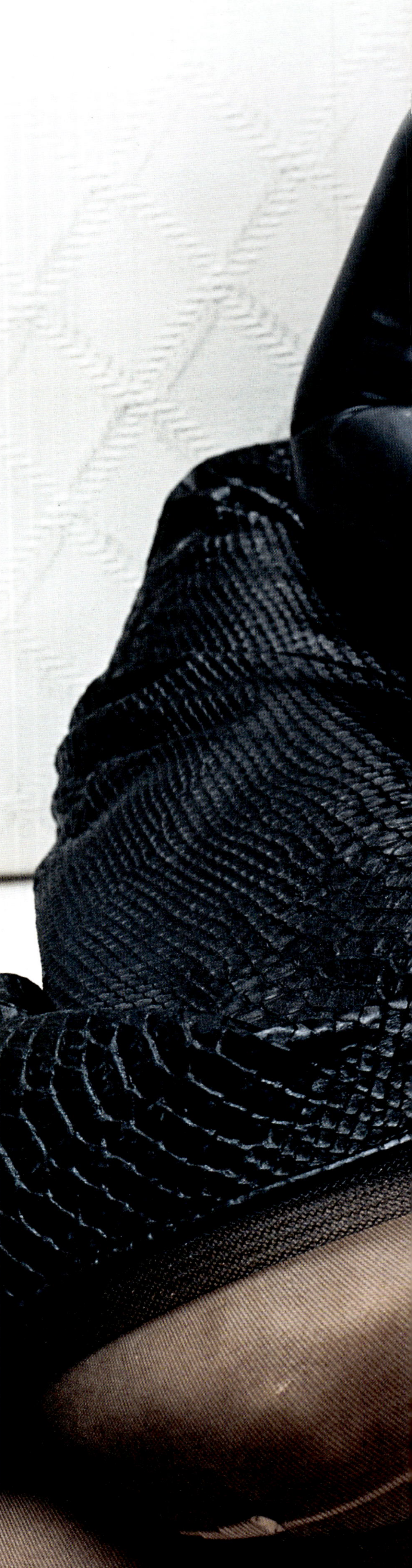

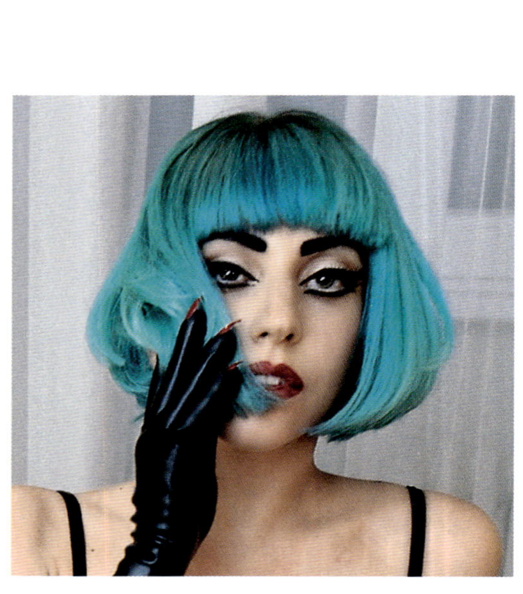

Sängerin Lady Gaga, Köln, 2011
The singer Lady Gaga, Cologne, 2011

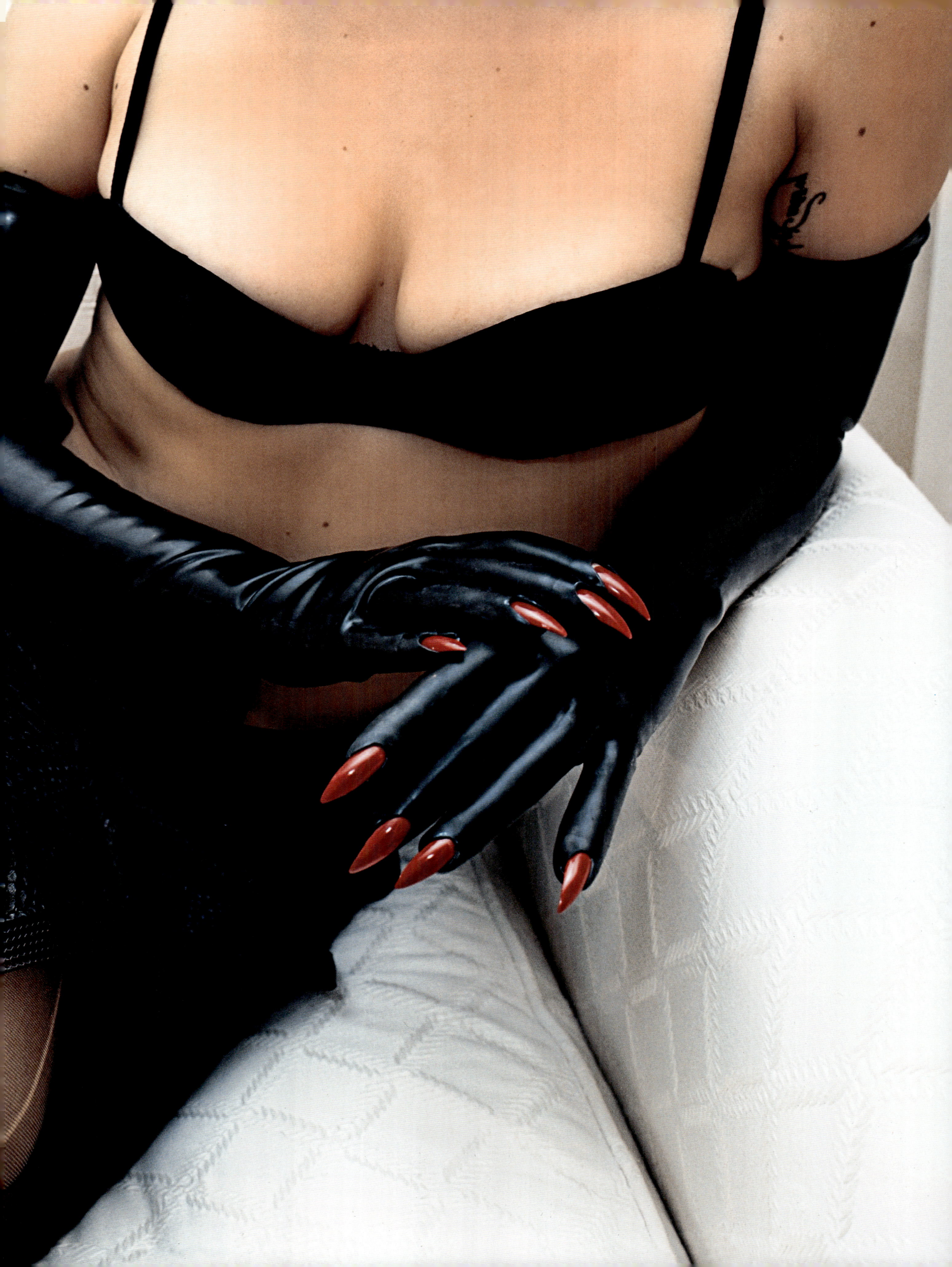

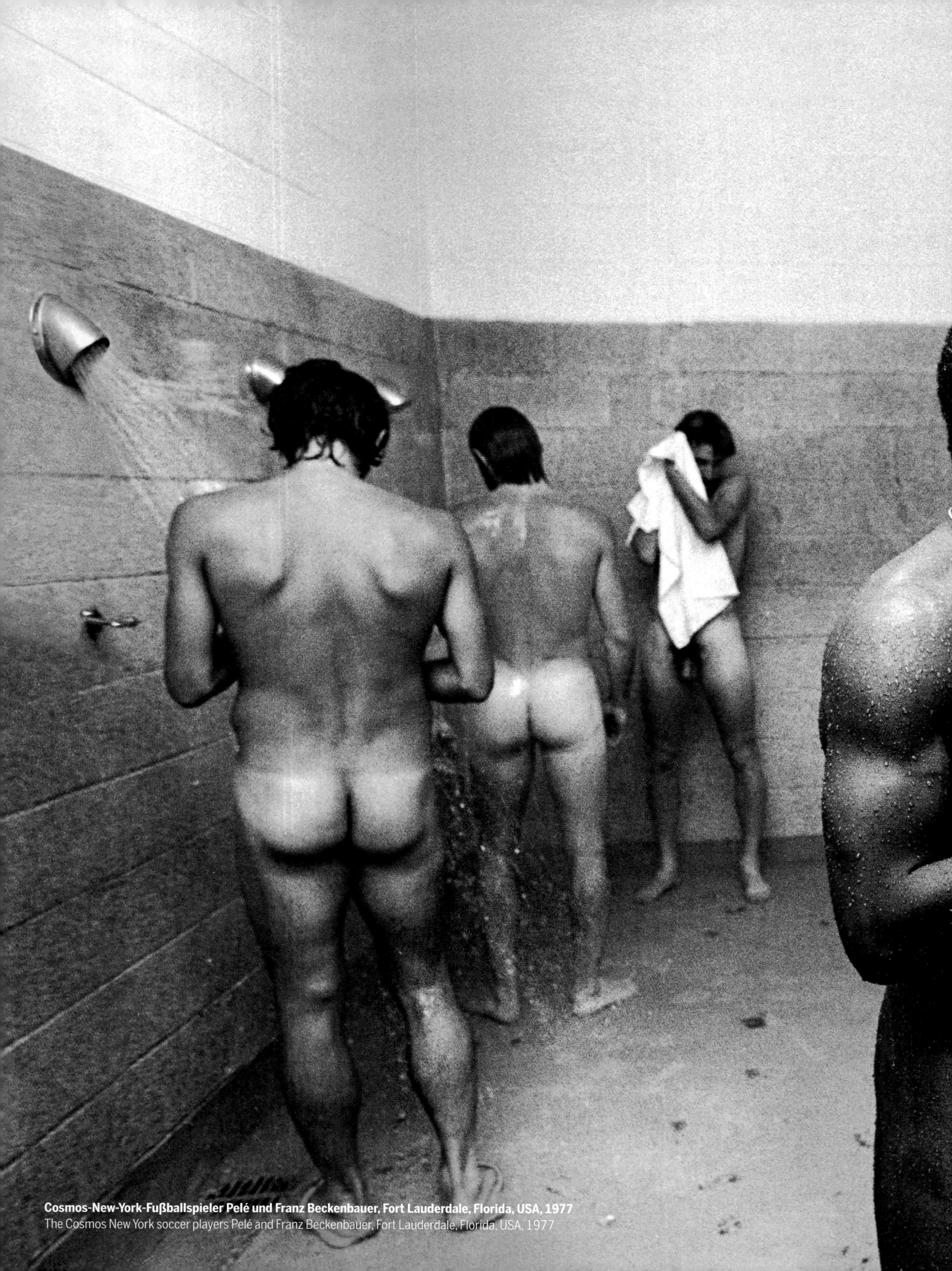

Cosmos-New-York-Fußballspieler Pelé und Franz Beckenbauer, Fort Lauderdale, Florida, USA, 1977
The Cosmos New York soccer players Pelé and Franz Beckenbauer, Fort Lauderdale, Florida, USA, 1977

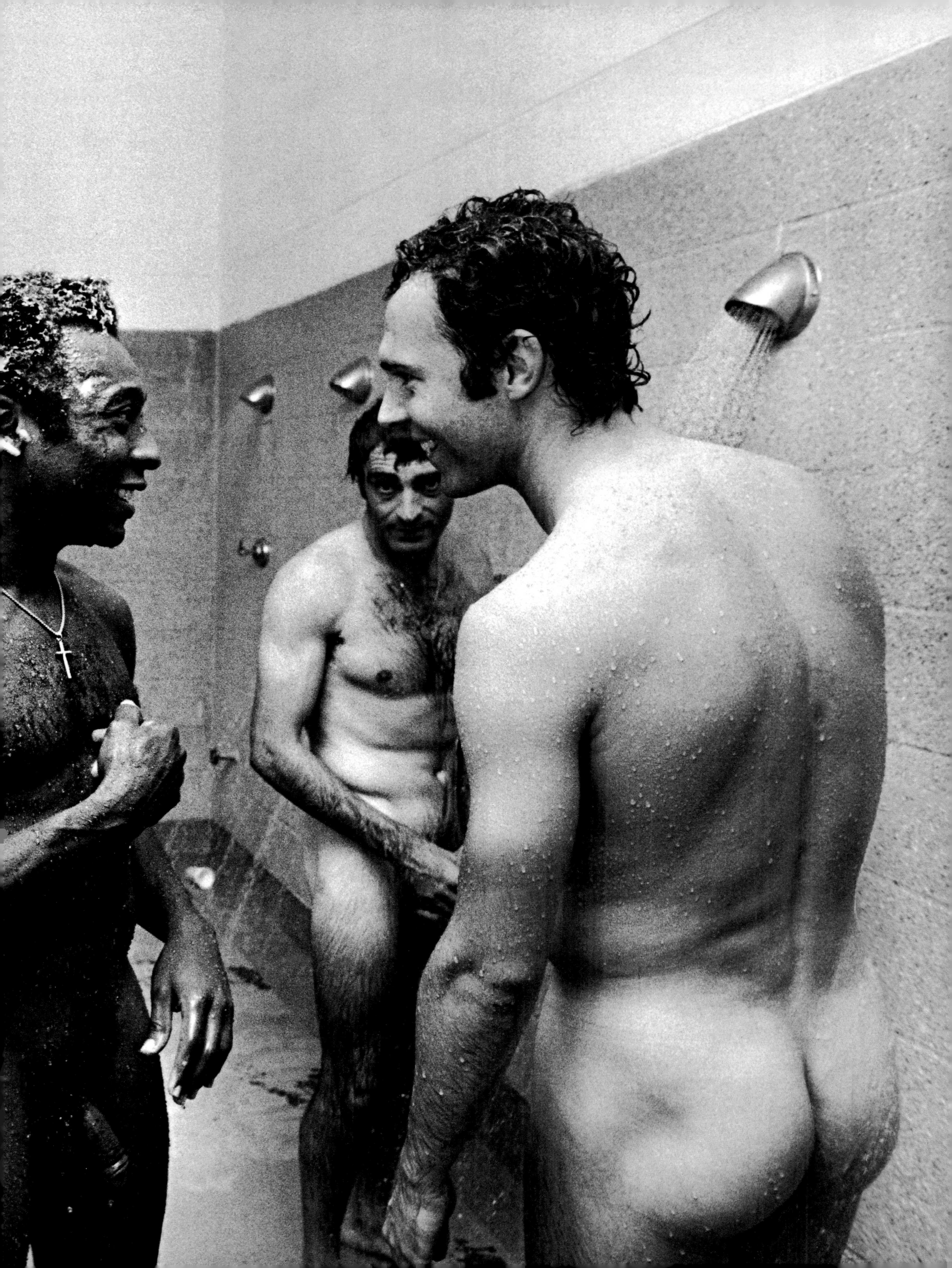

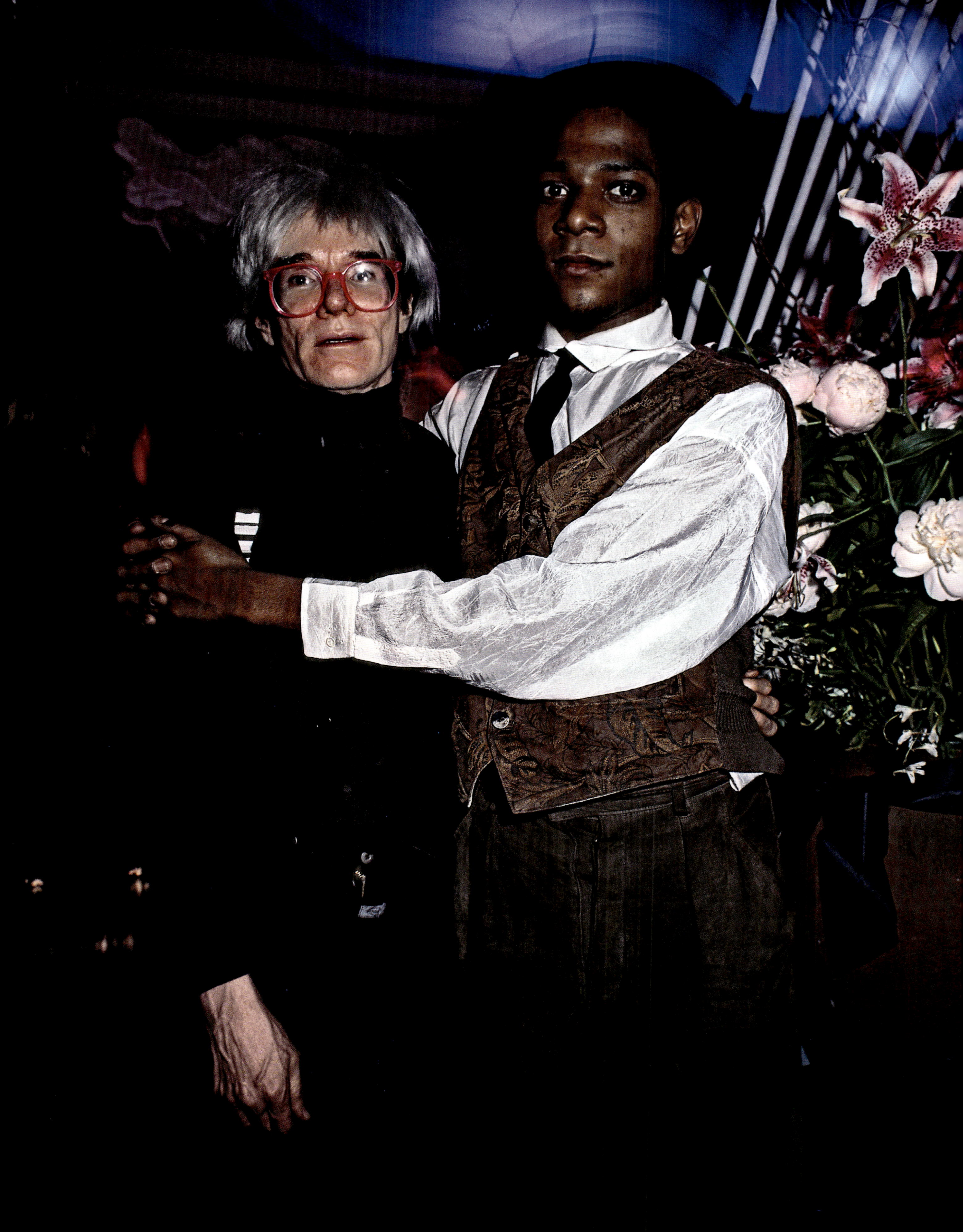

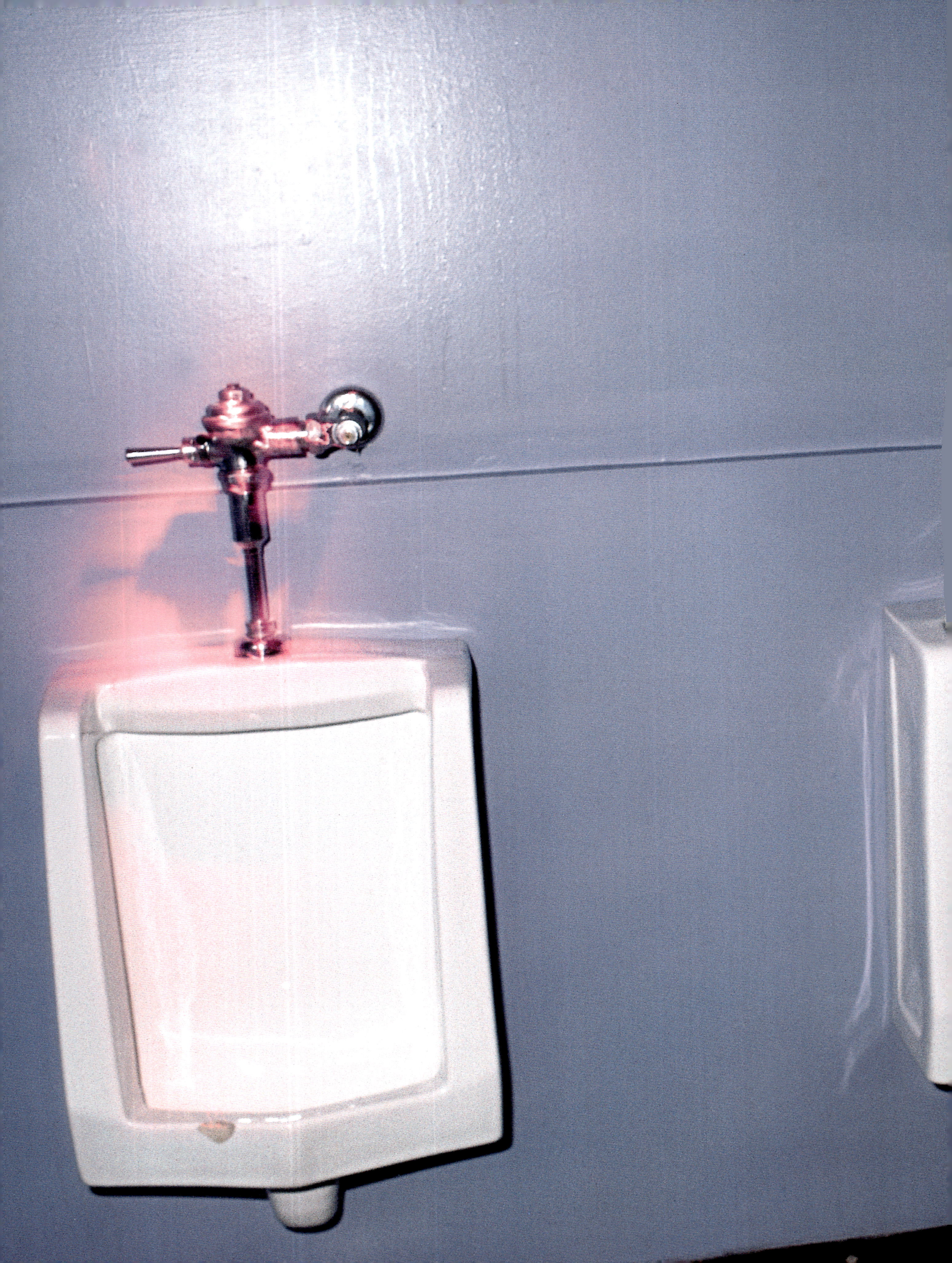

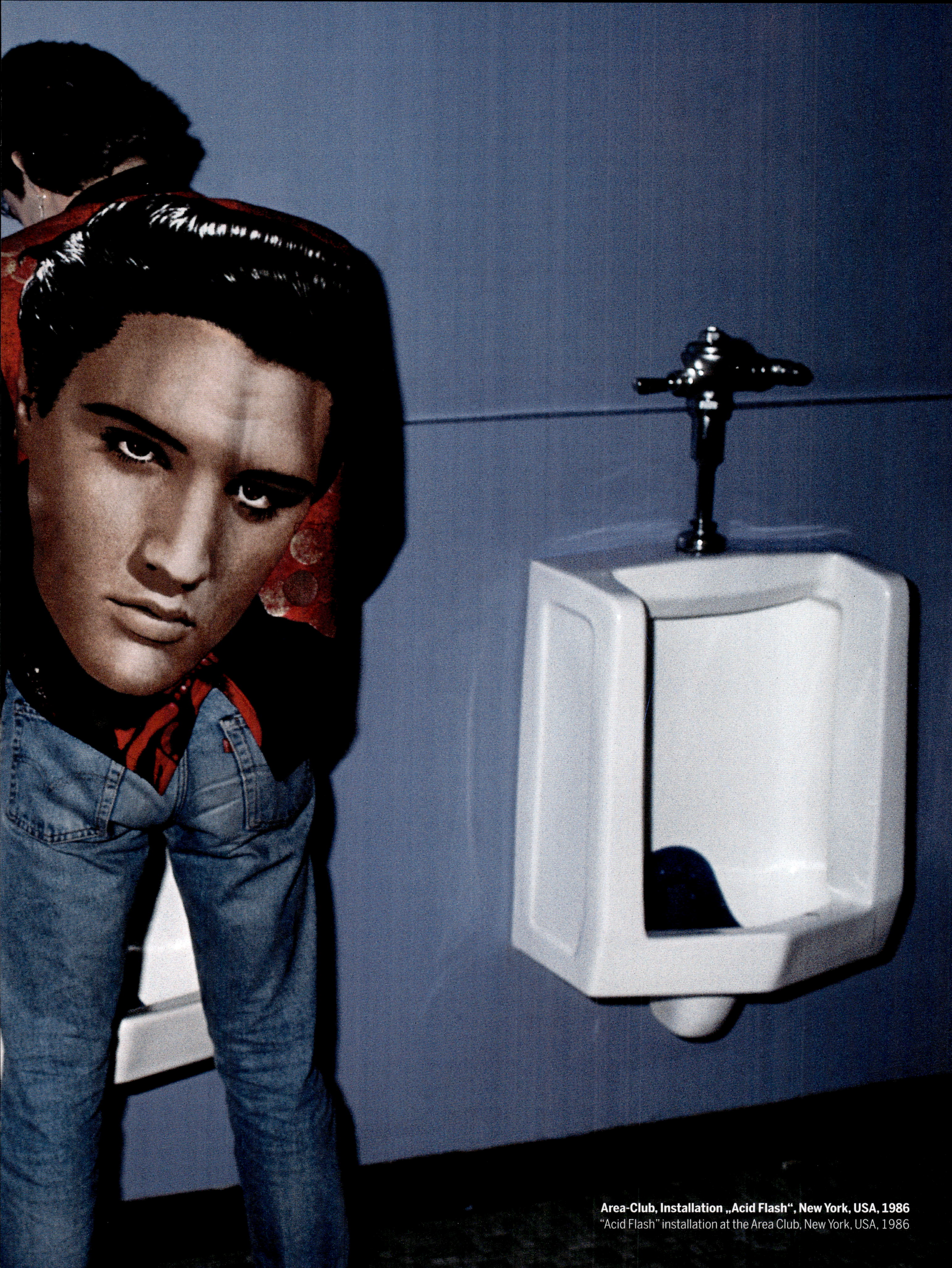

Area-Club, Installation „Acid Flash", New York, USA, 1986
"Acid Flash" installation at the Area Club, New York, USA, 1986

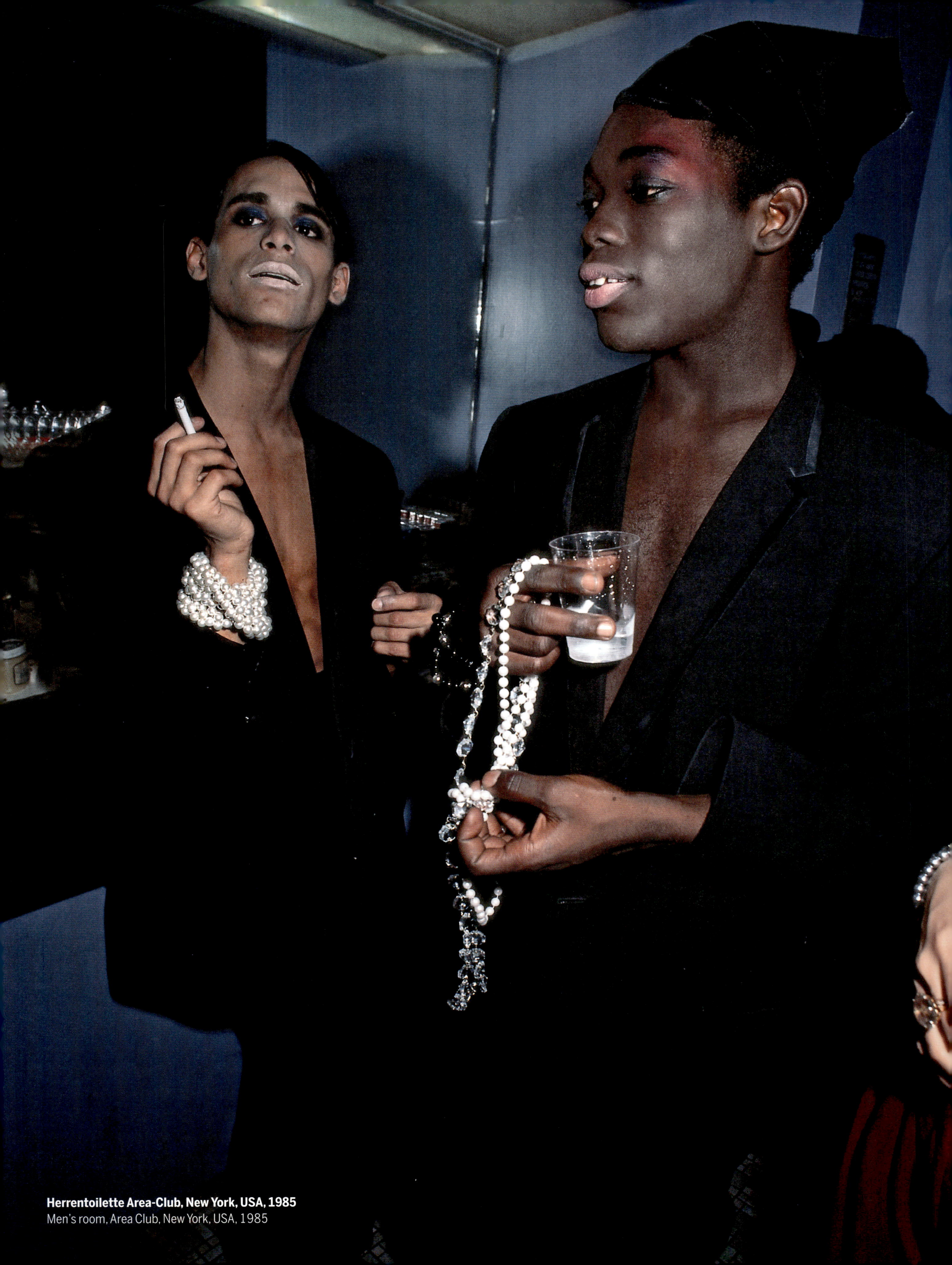

Herrentoilette Area-Club, New York, USA, 1985
Men's room, Area Club, New York, USA, 1985

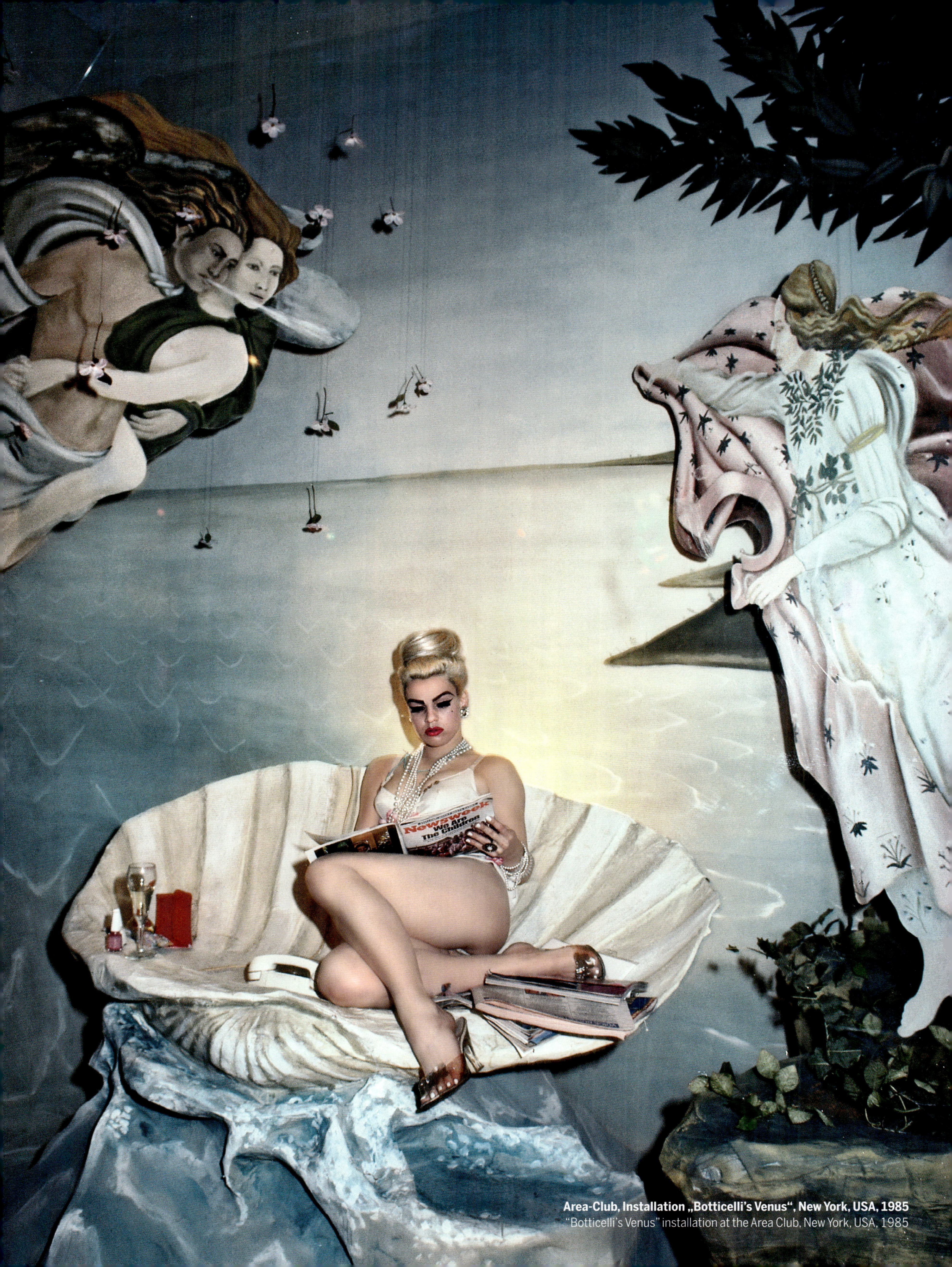

Area-Club, Installation „Botticelli's Venus", New York, USA, 1985
"Botticelli's Venus" installation at the Area Club, New York, USA, 1985

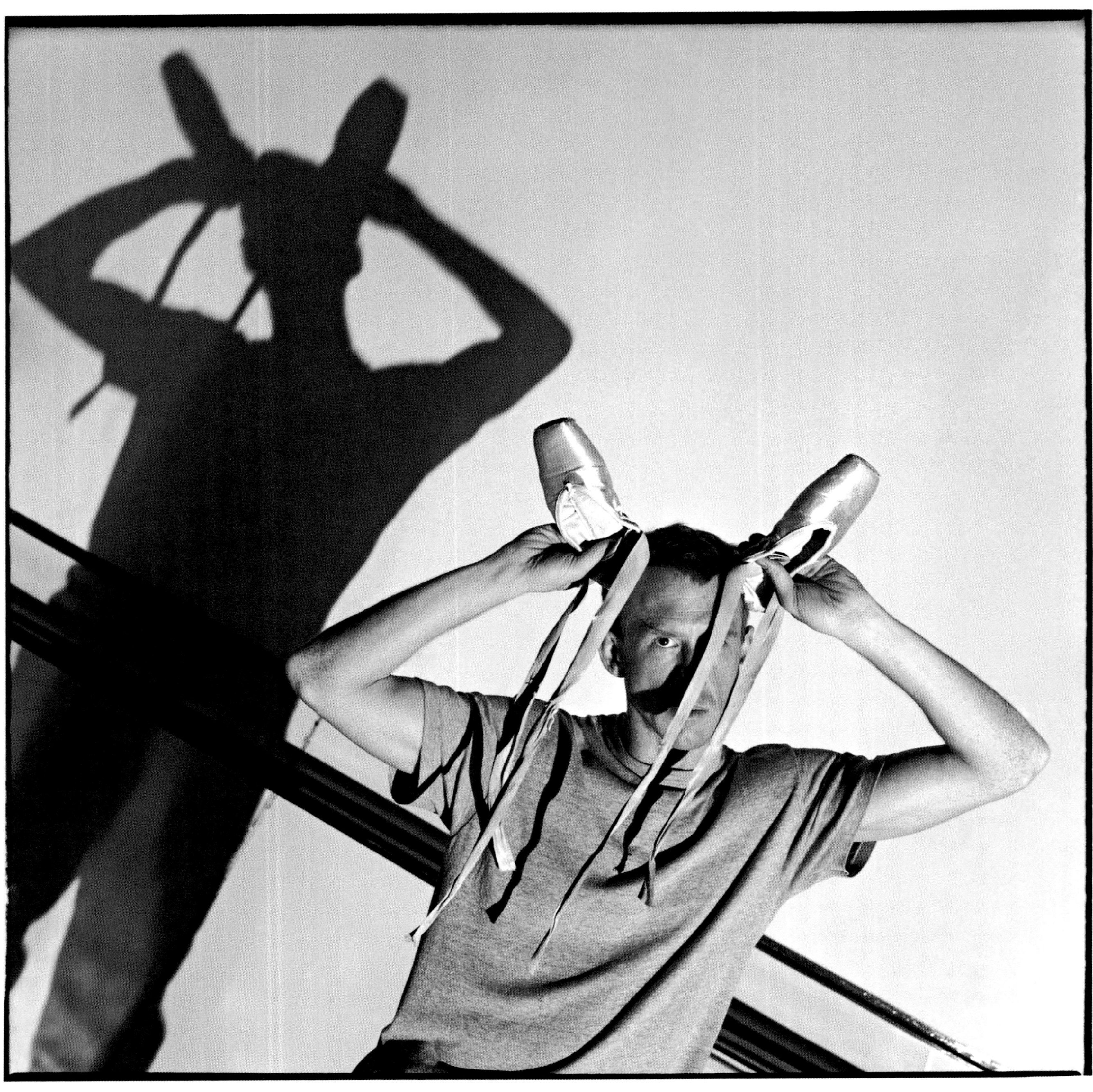

Choreograf und Intendant William Forsythe, Frankfurt, 1989
The choreographer and artistic director William Forsythe, Frankfurt, 1989

Tänzer der Forsythe Company, Frankfurt, 1989
A Forsythe Company dancer, Frankfurt, 1989

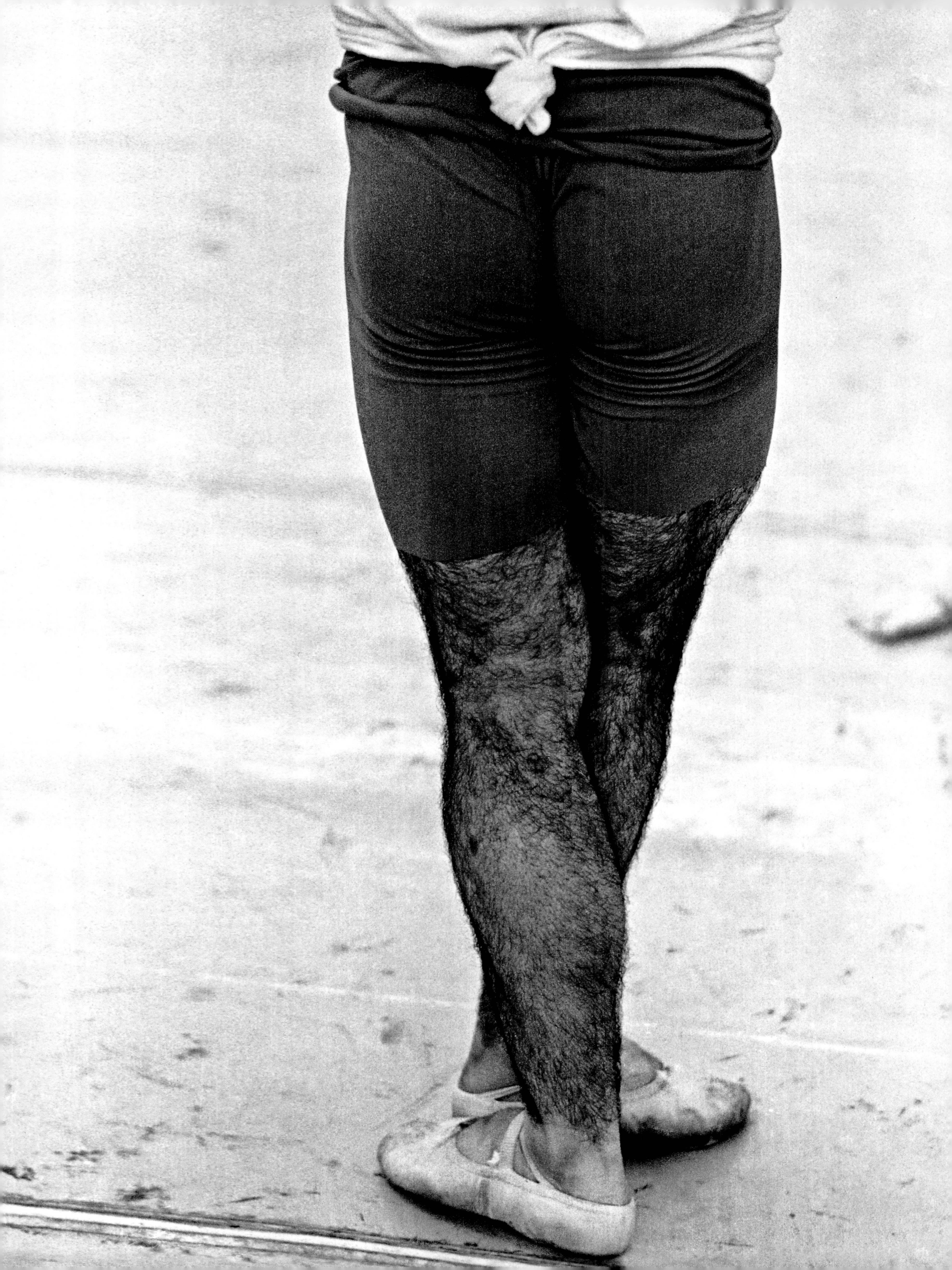

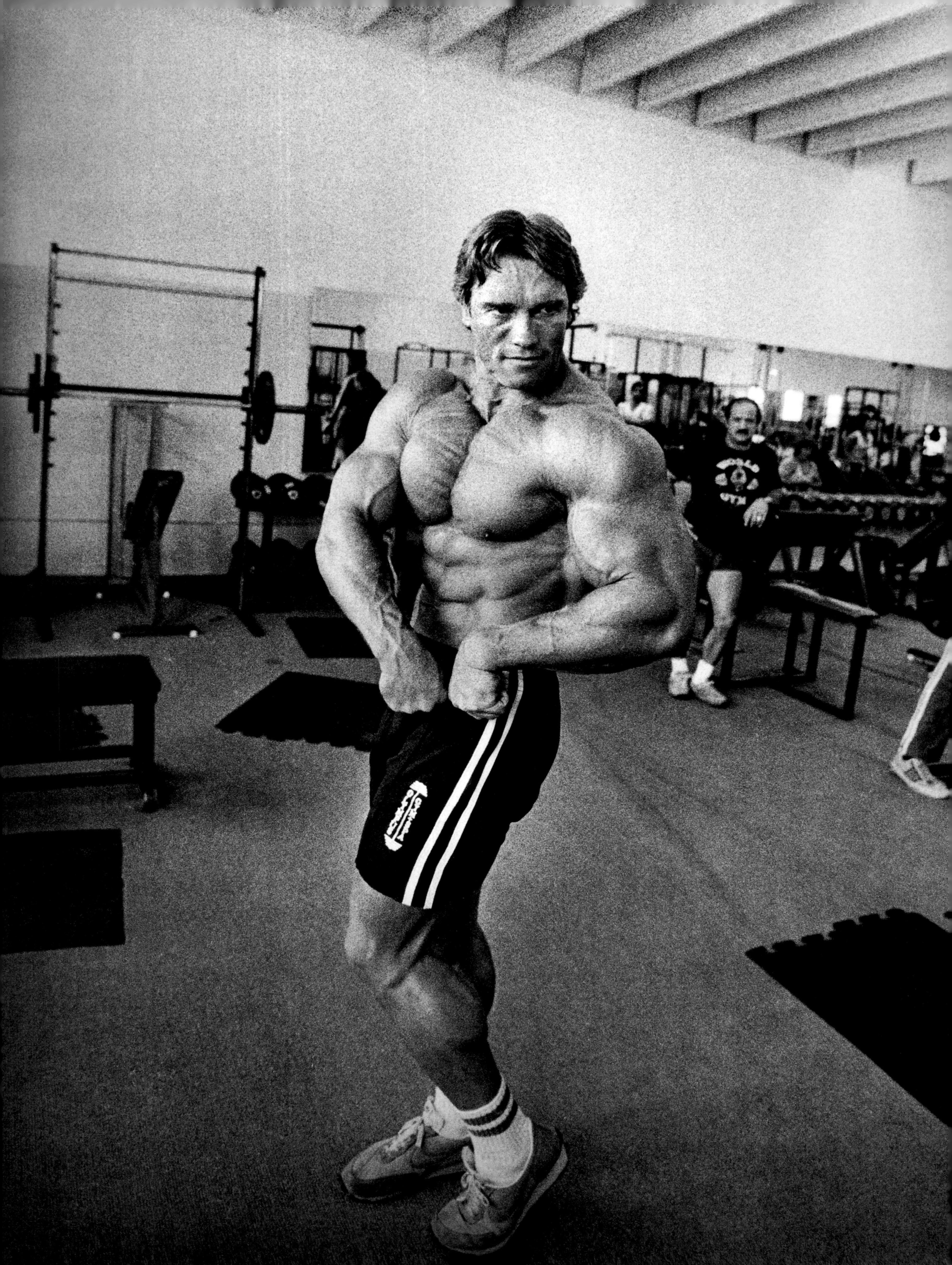

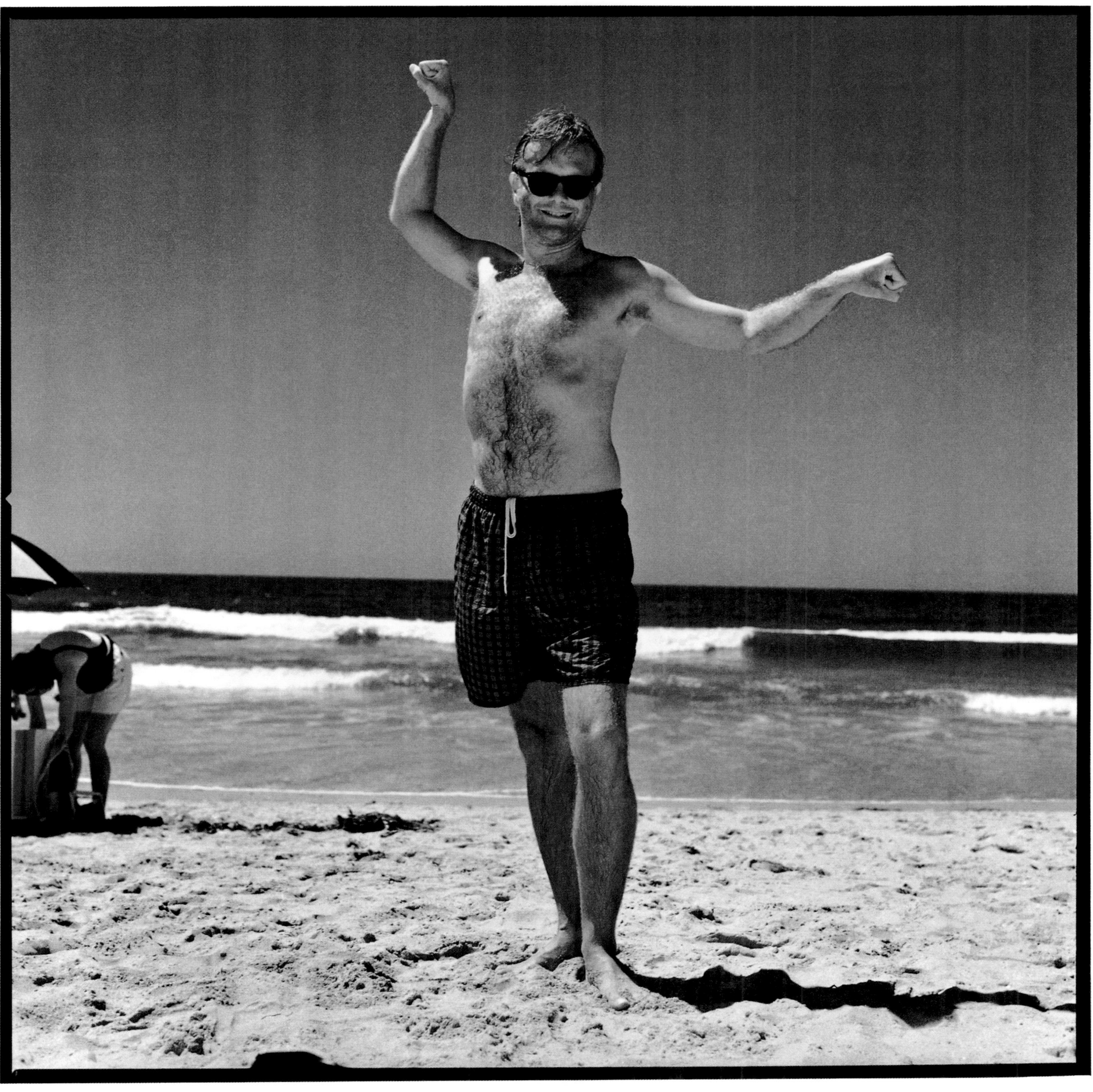

Entertainer Harald Schmidt, Santa Monica, Kalifornien, USA, 1997
The entertainer Harald Schmidt, Santa Monica, California, USA, 1997

Bodybuilder und Schauspieler Arnold Schwarzenegger, Santa Monica, Kalifornien, USA, 1980
The bodybuilder and actor Arnold Schwarzenegger, Santa Monica, California, USA, 1980

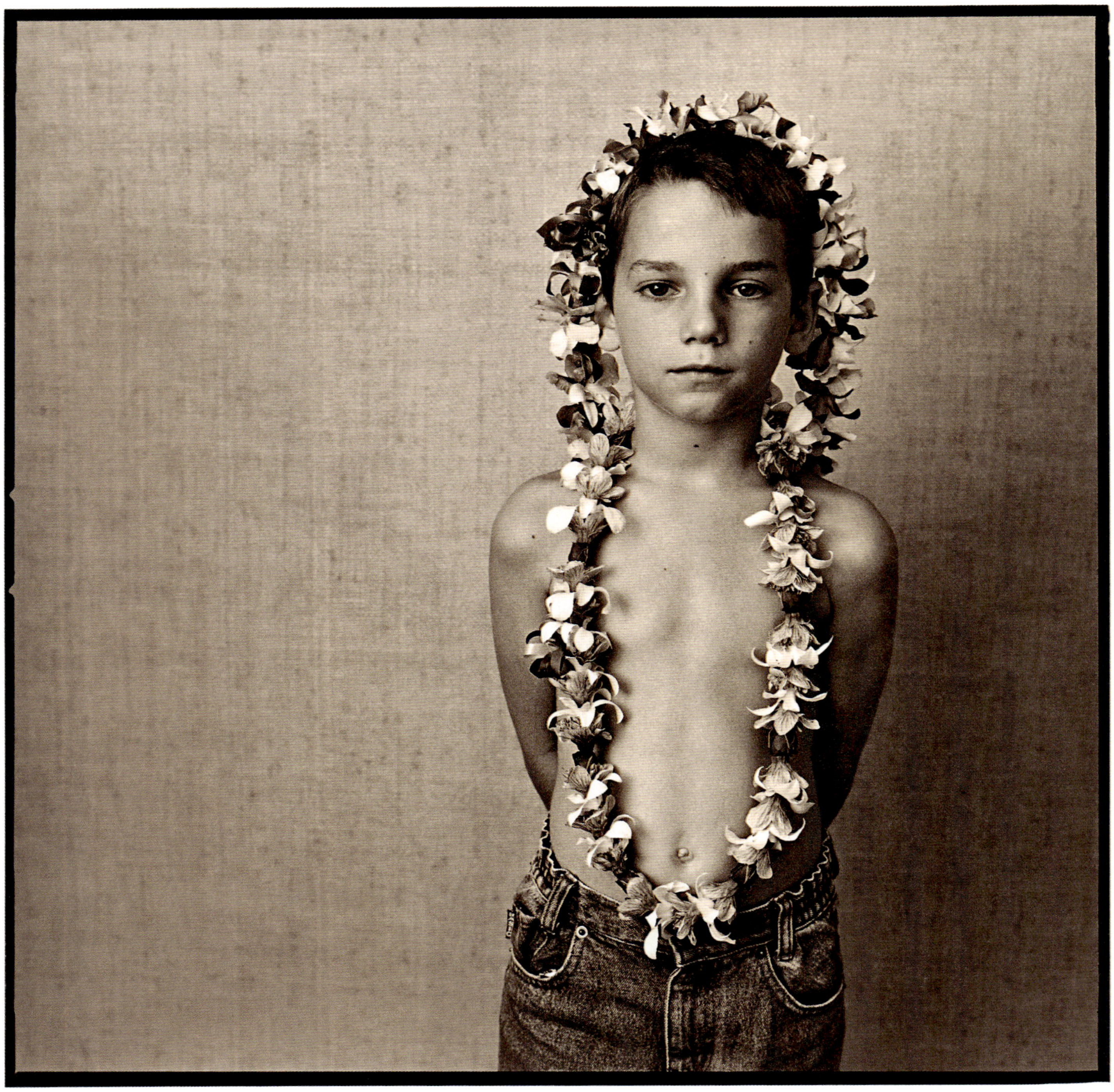

Theodor Hinz, Big Island, Hawaii, USA, 1999
Theodor Hinz, Big Island, Hawaii, USA, 1999

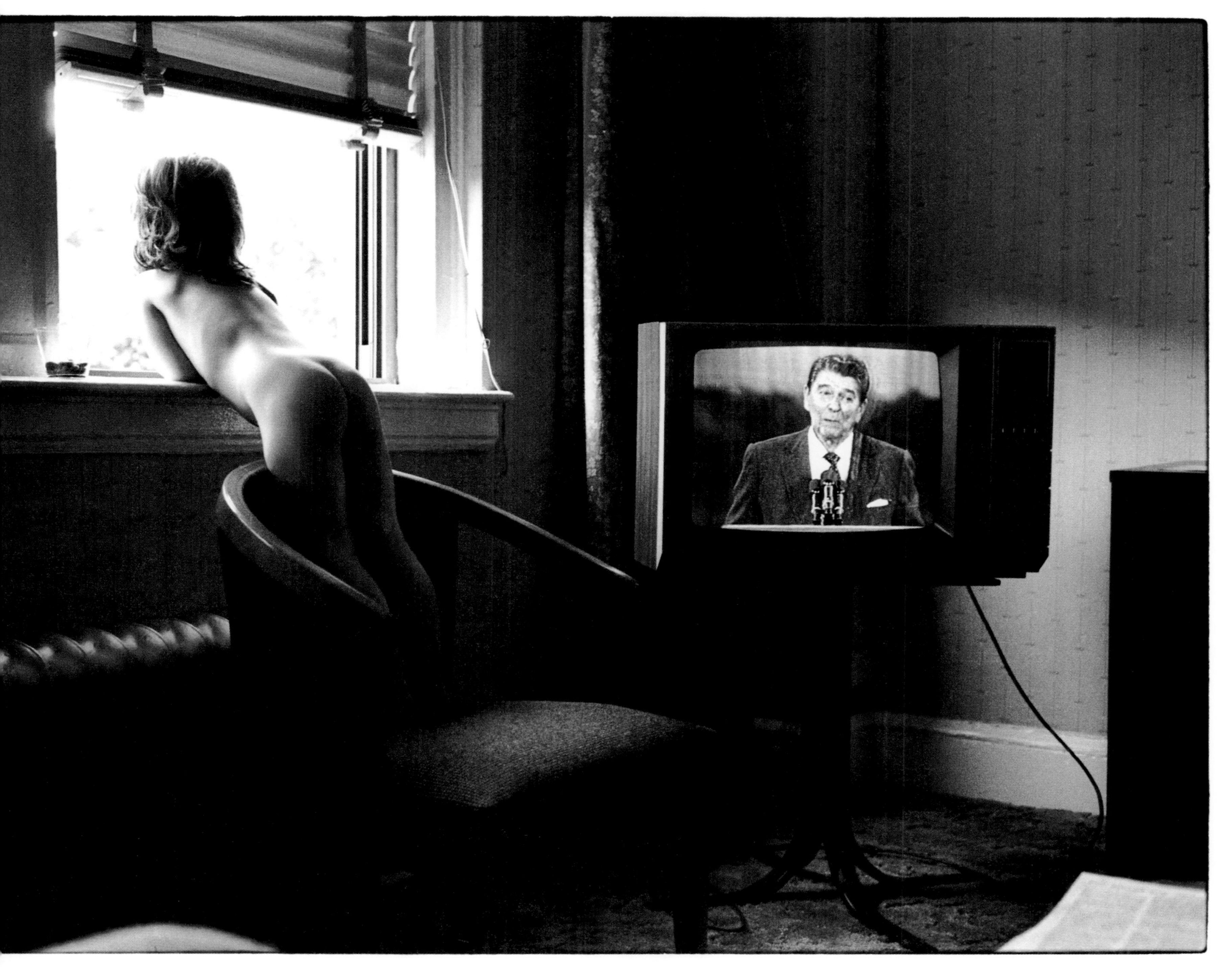

Hotel Excelsior, New York, USA, 1988
Hotel Excelsior, New York, USA, 1988

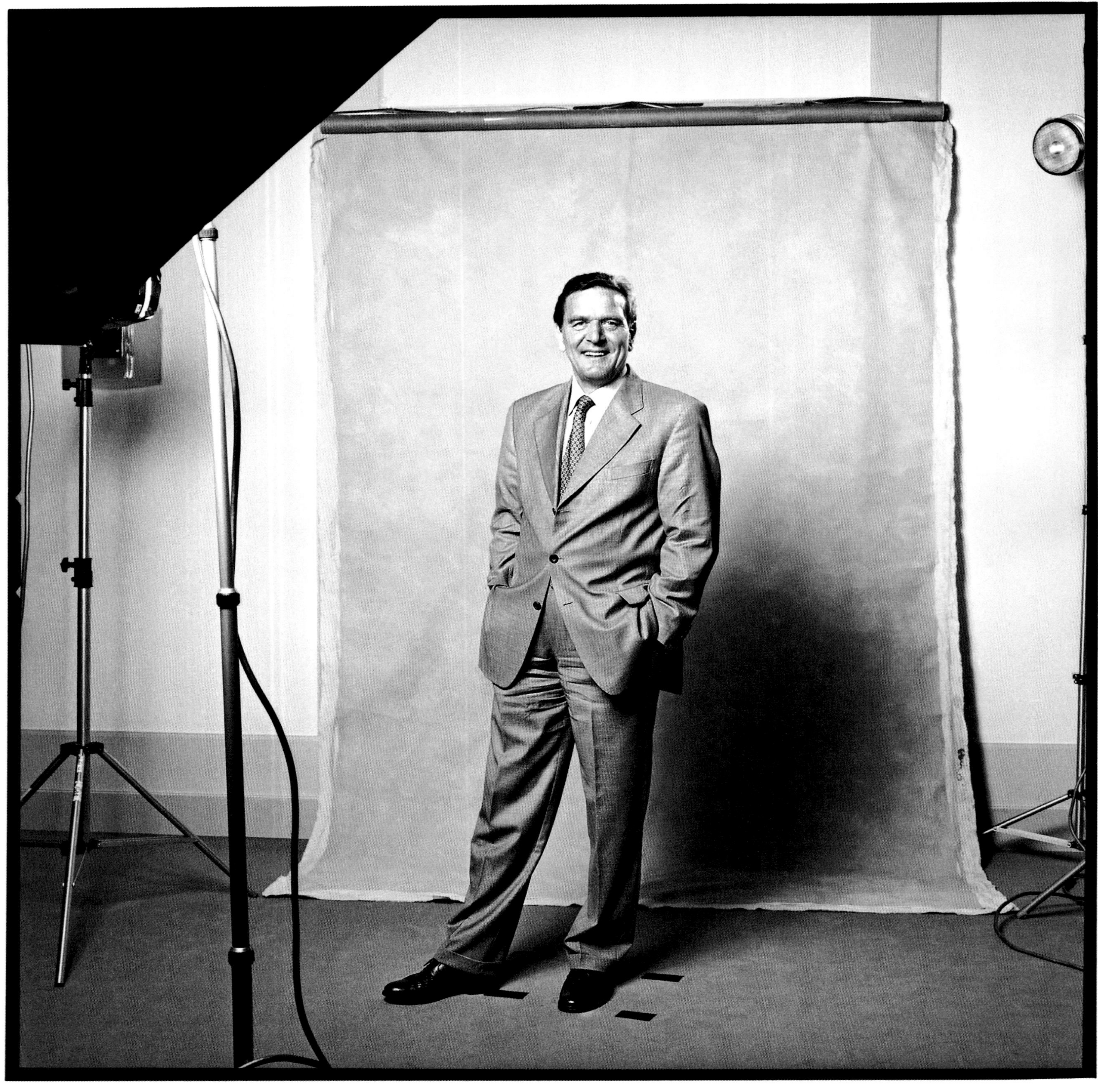

Politiker Gerhard Schröder, Hannover, 1997
The politician Gerhard Schröder, Hannover, 1997

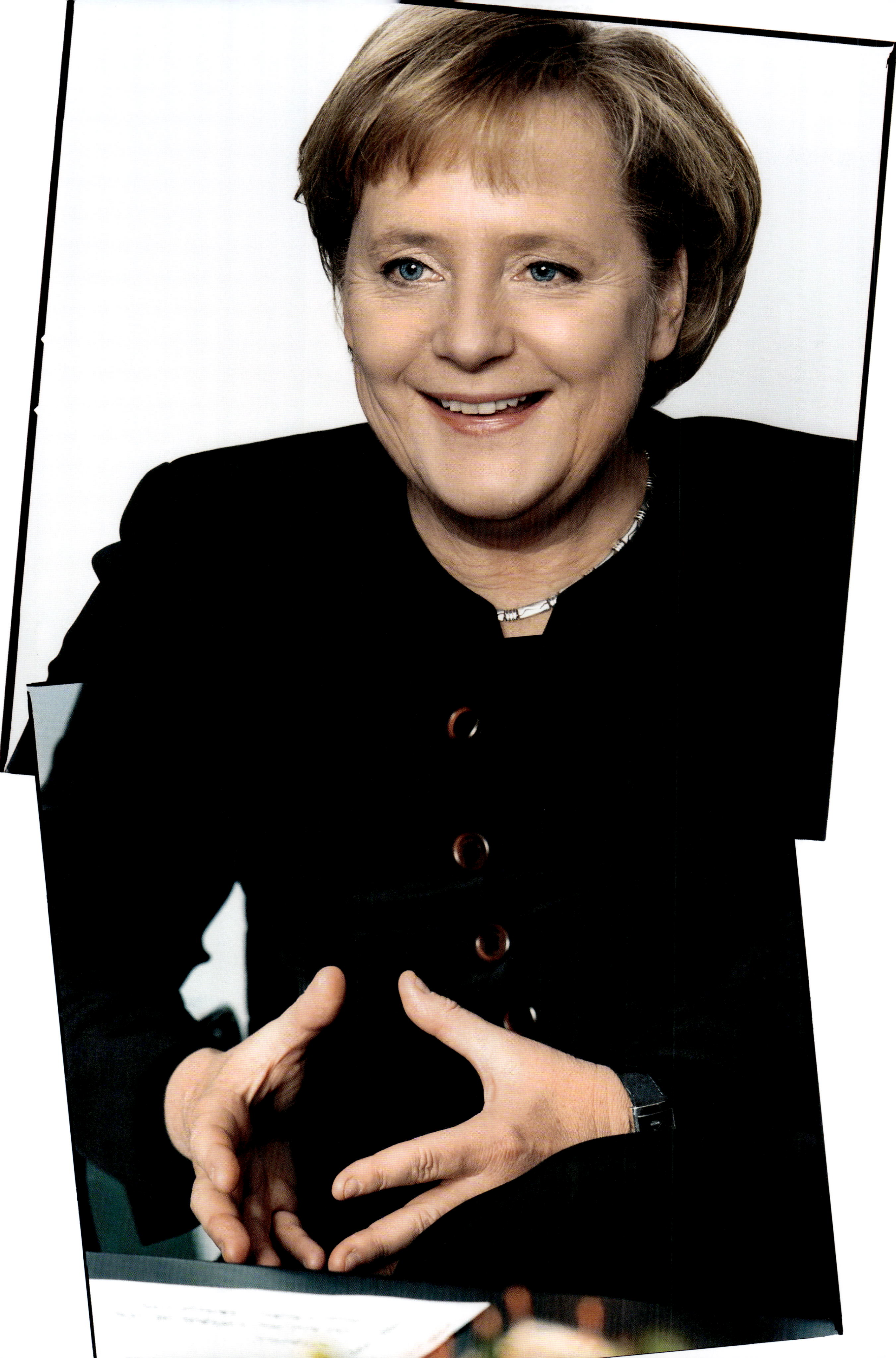

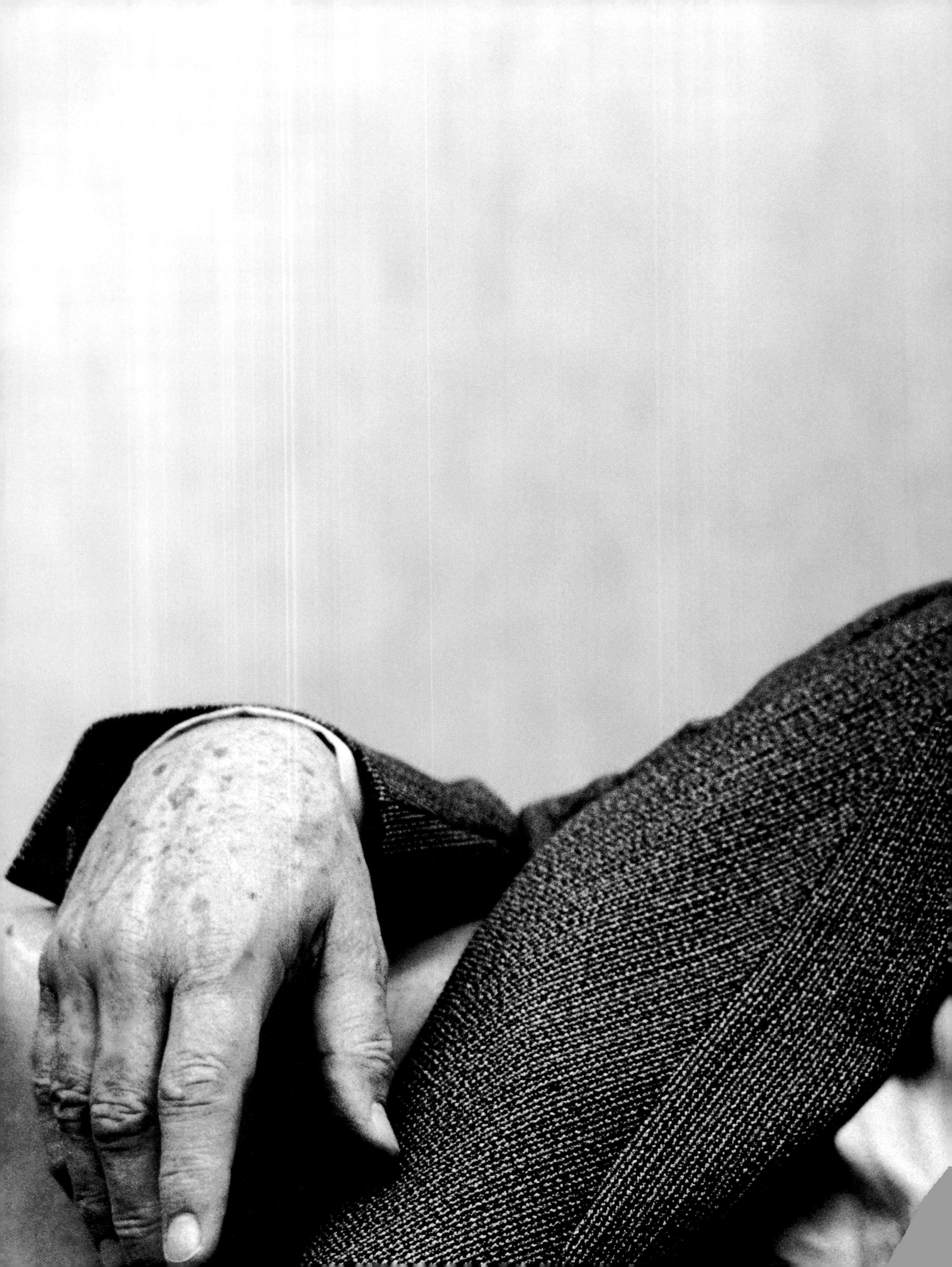

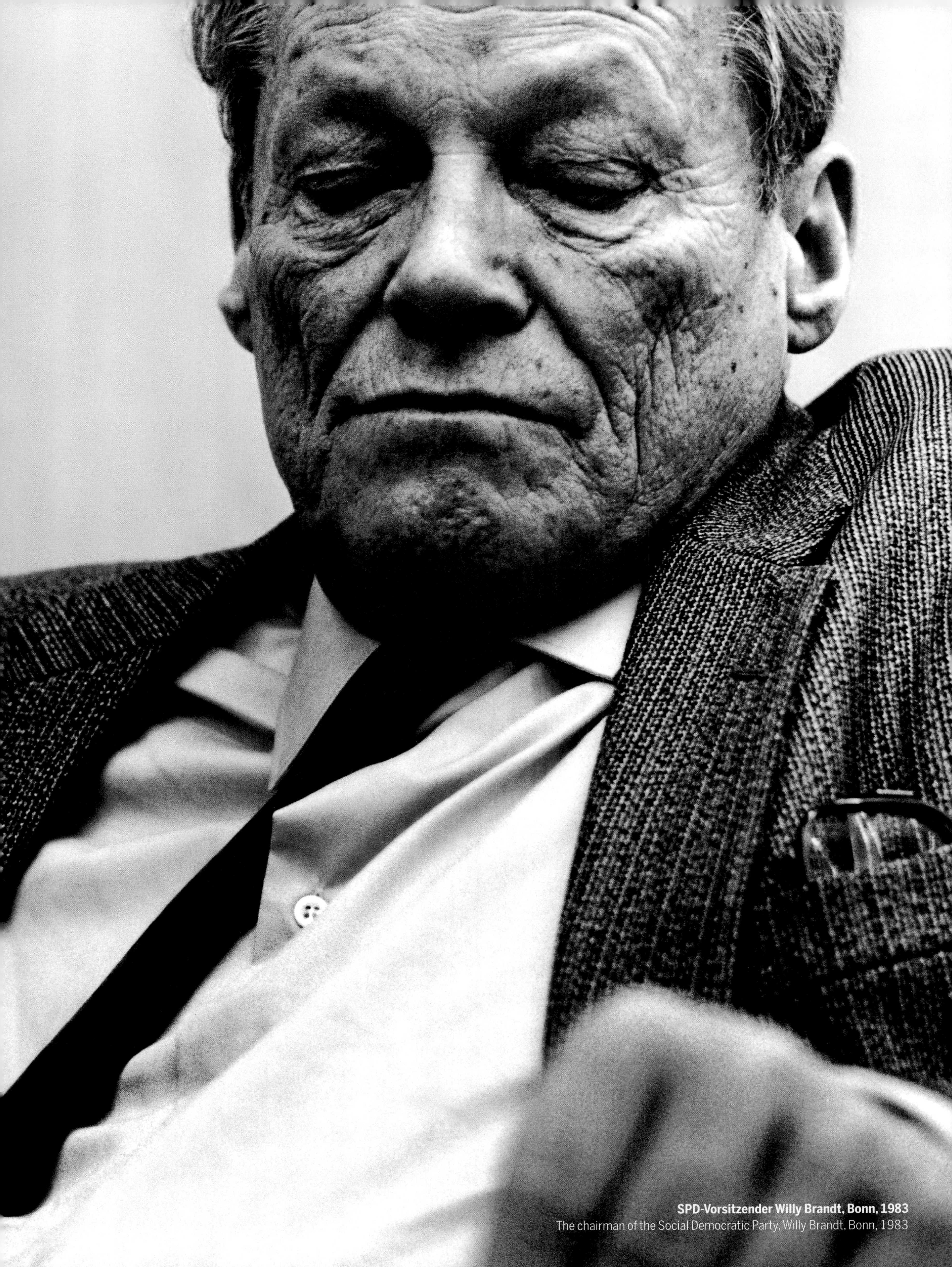

SPD-Vorsitzender Willy Brandt, Bonn, 1983
The chairman of the Social Democratic Party, Willy Brandt, Bonn, 1983

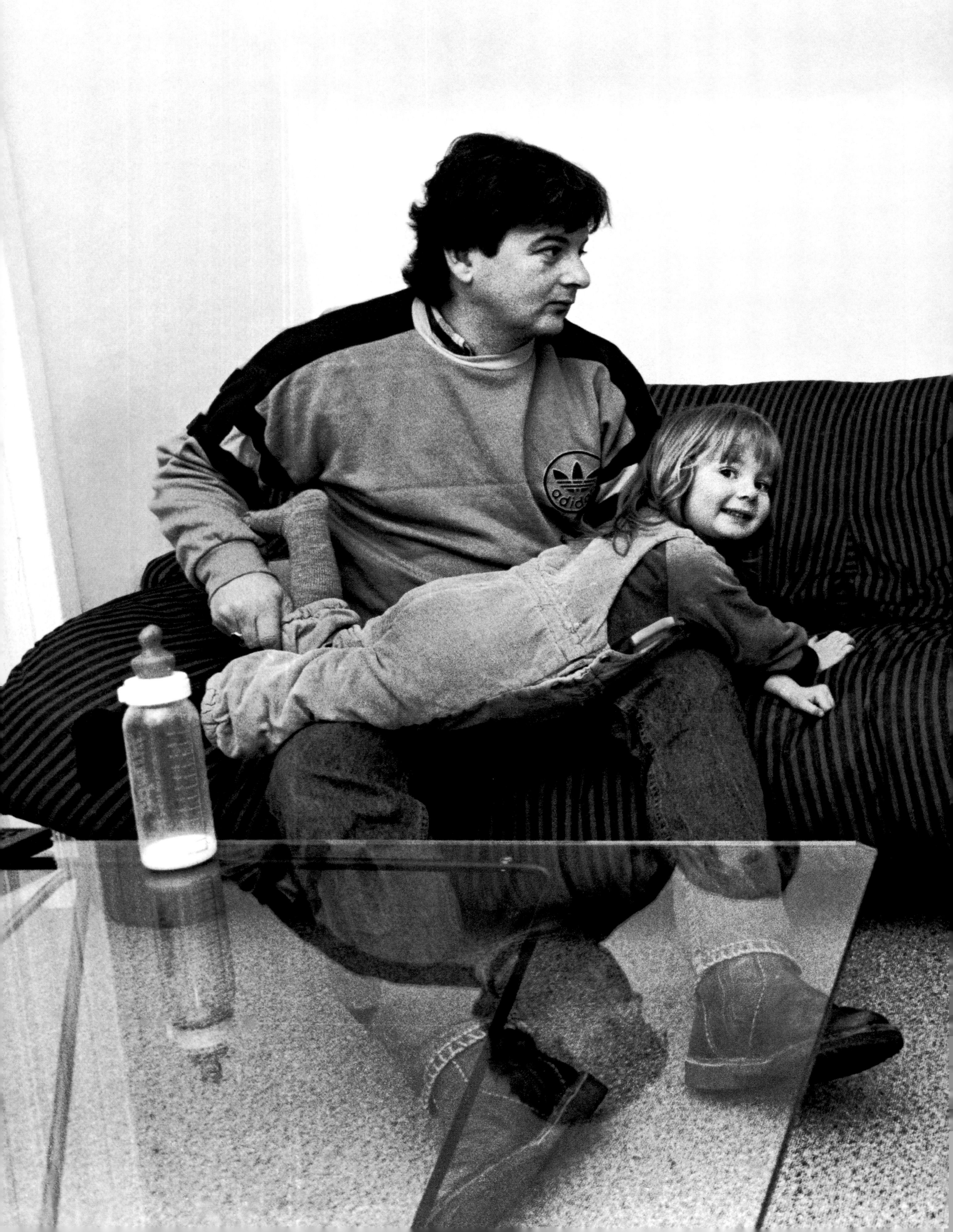

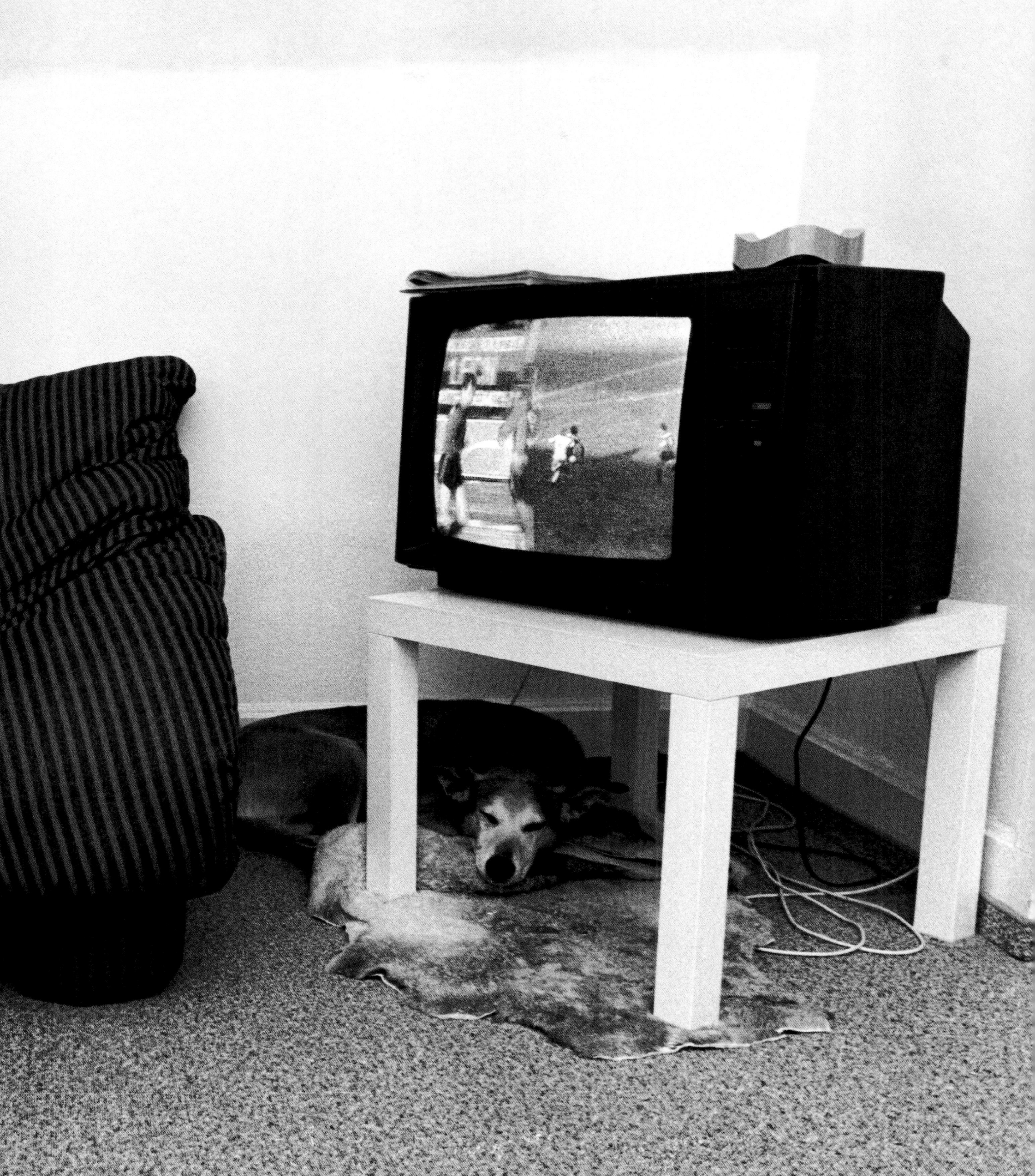

Grünen-Politiker Joschka Fischer mit Tochter und Hund, Frankfurt, 1987
The Greens' party politician Joschka Fischer with his daughter and dog, Frankfurt, 1987

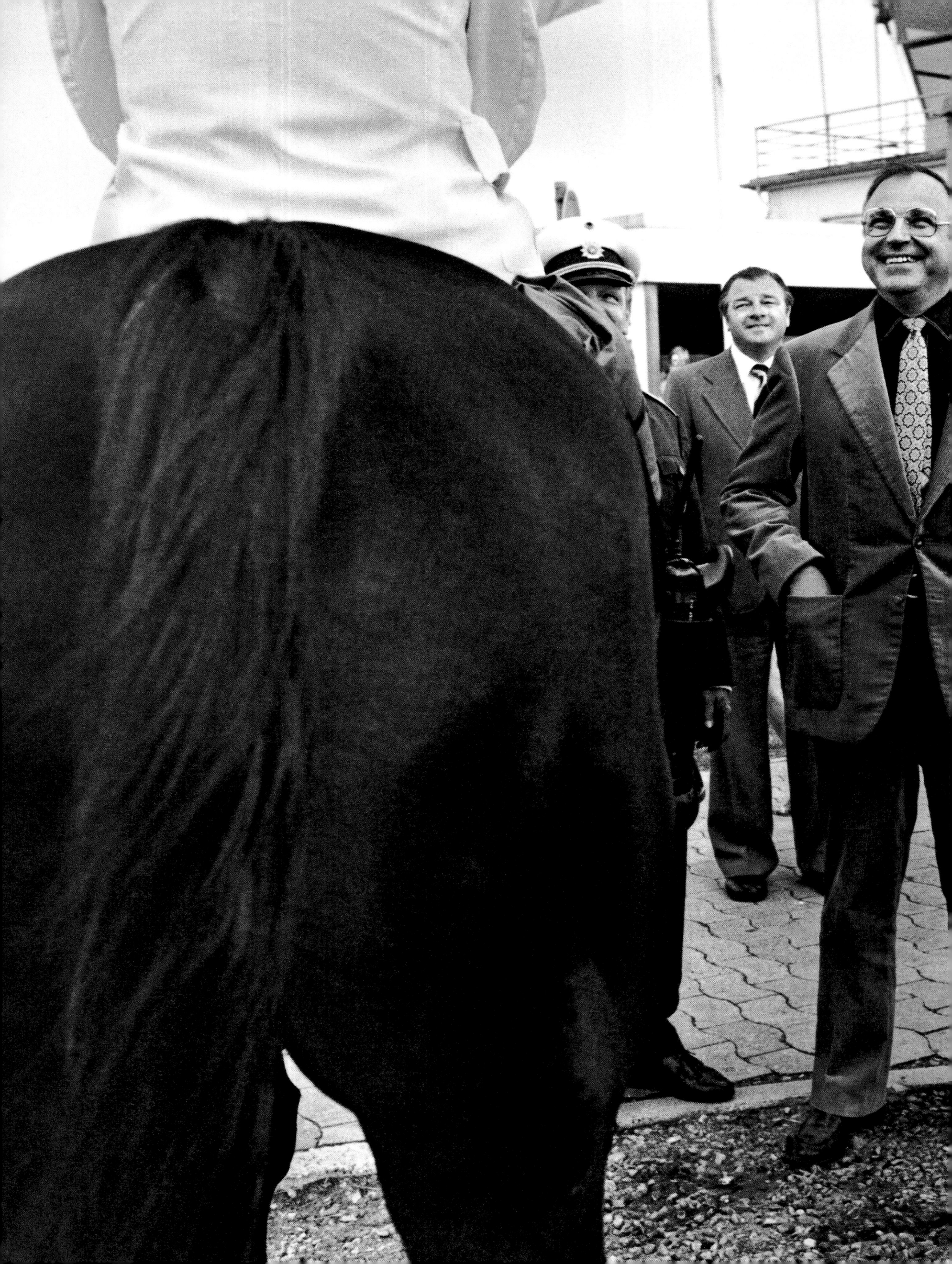

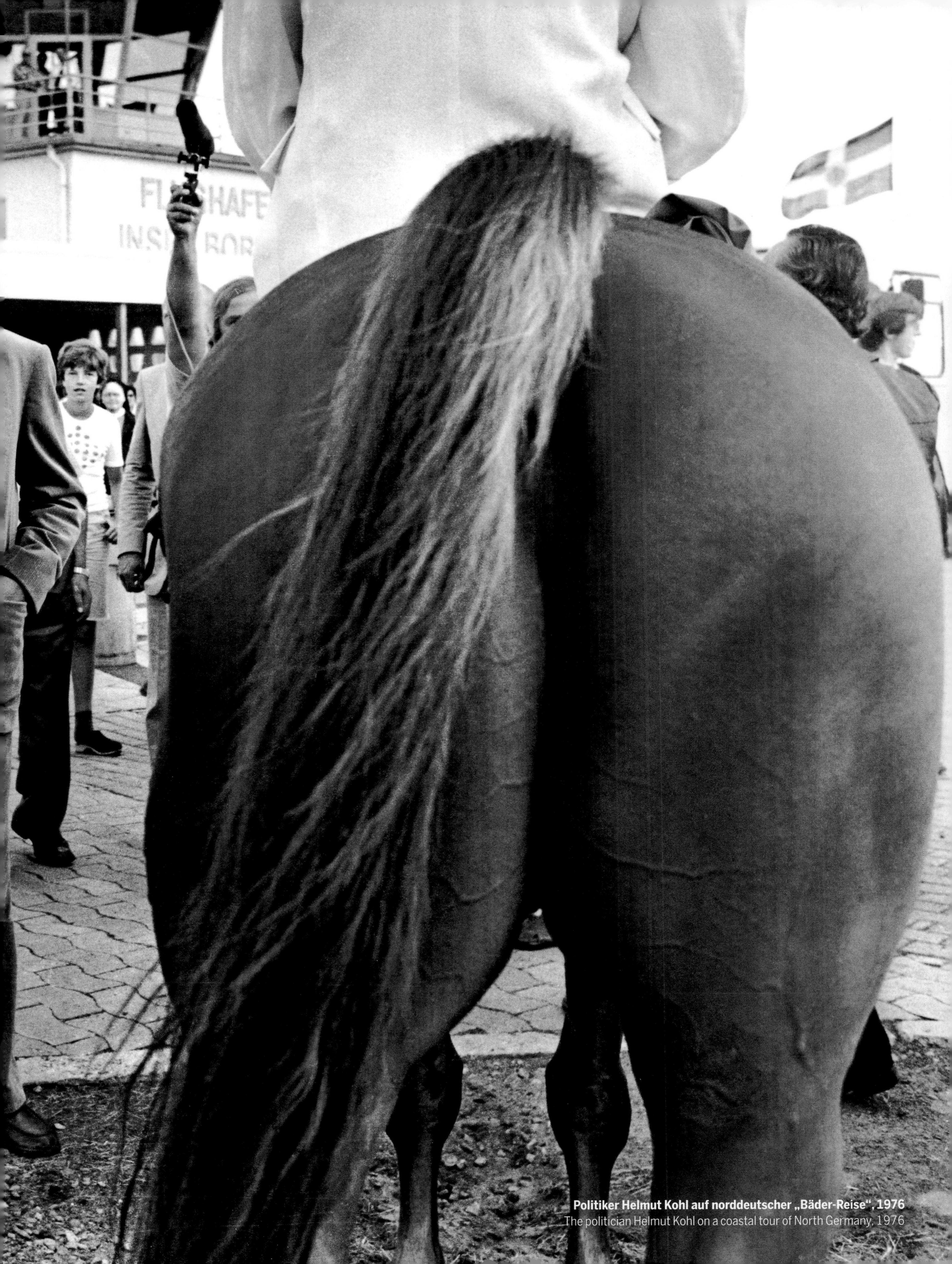

Politiker Helmut Kohl auf norddeutscher „Bäder-Reise", 1976
The politician Helmut Kohl on a coastal tour of North Germany, 1976

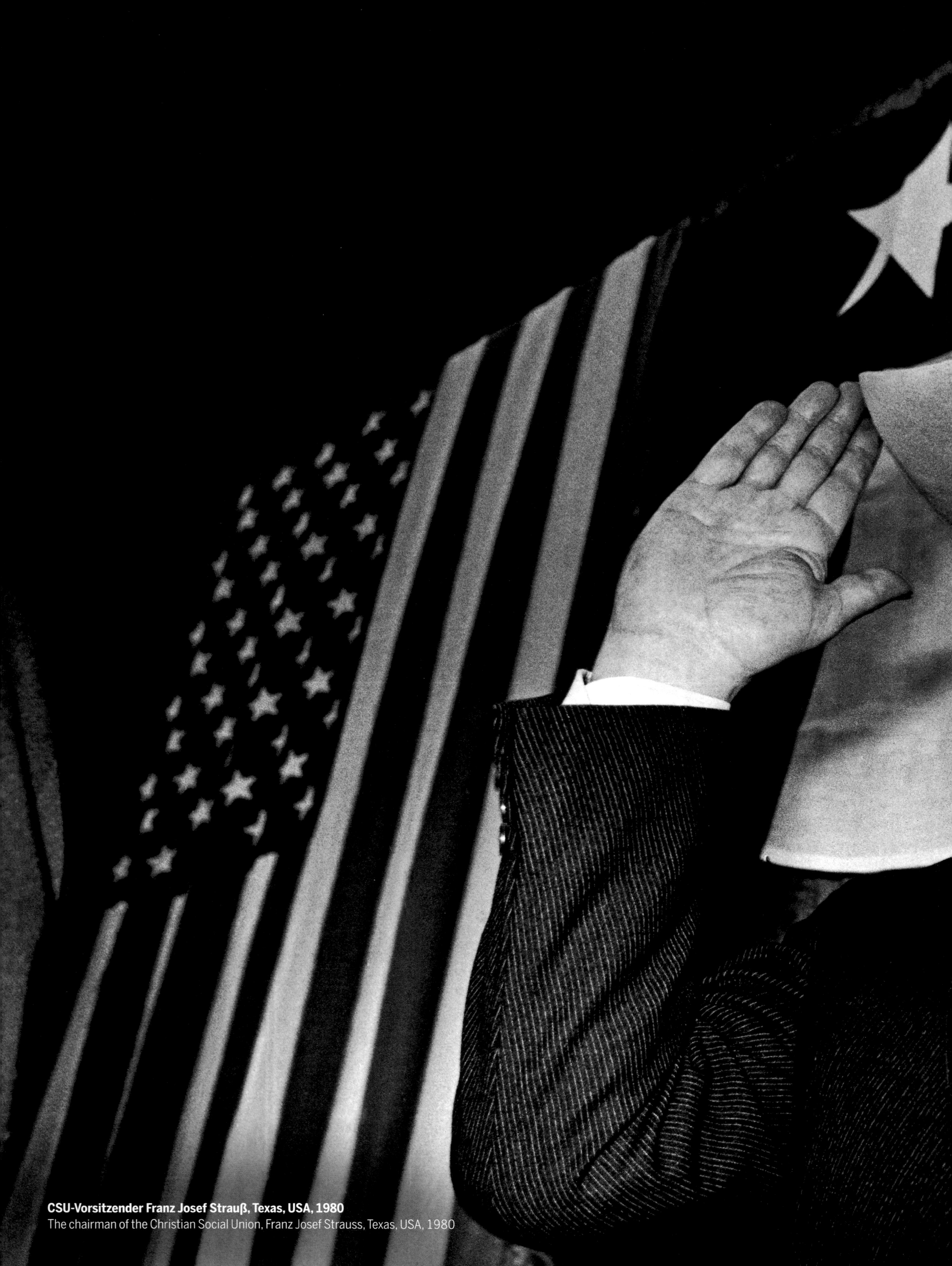

CSU-Vorsitzender Franz Josef Strauß, Texas, USA, 1980
The chairman of the Christian Social Union, Franz Josef Strauss, Texas, USA, 1980

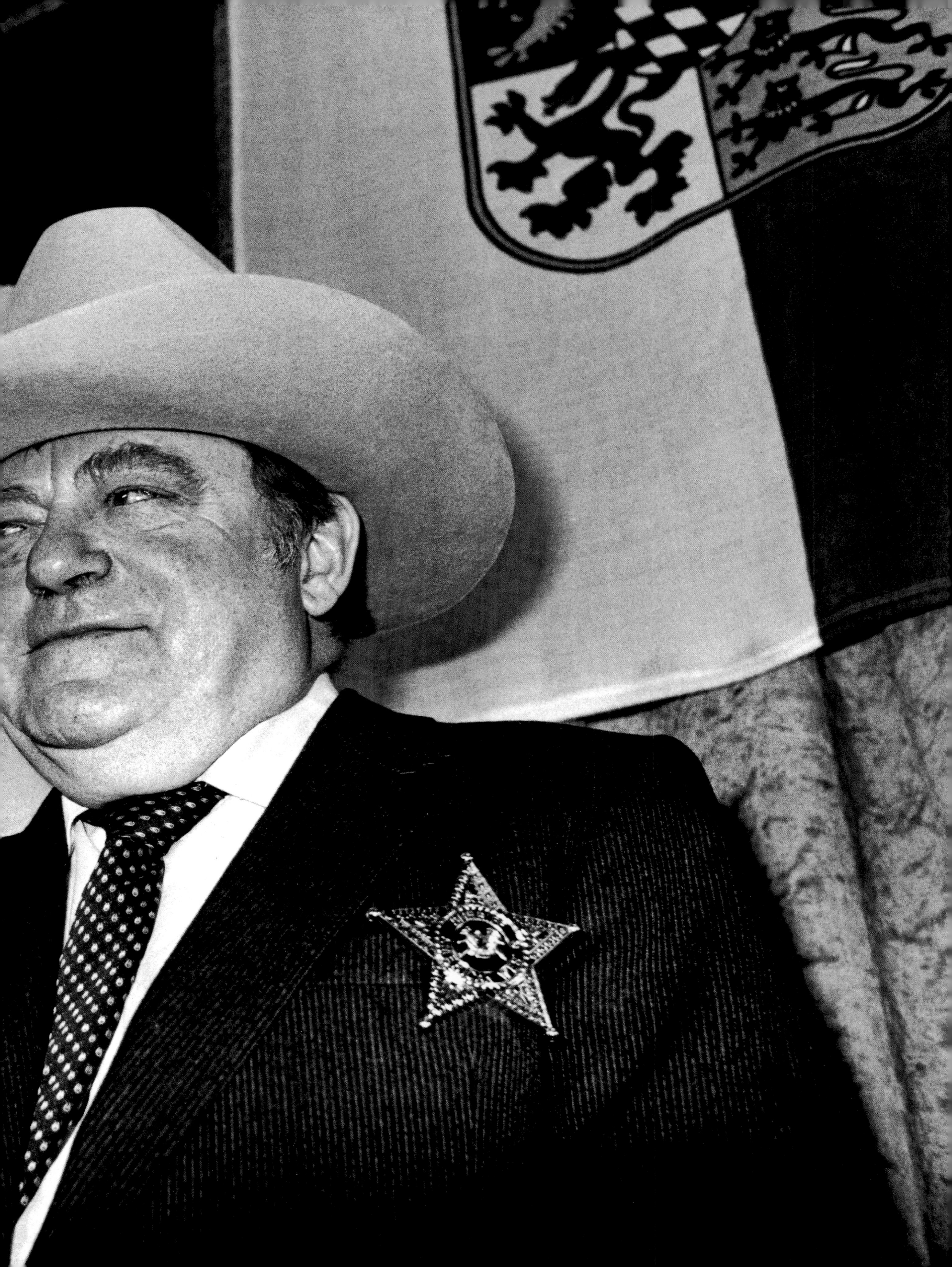

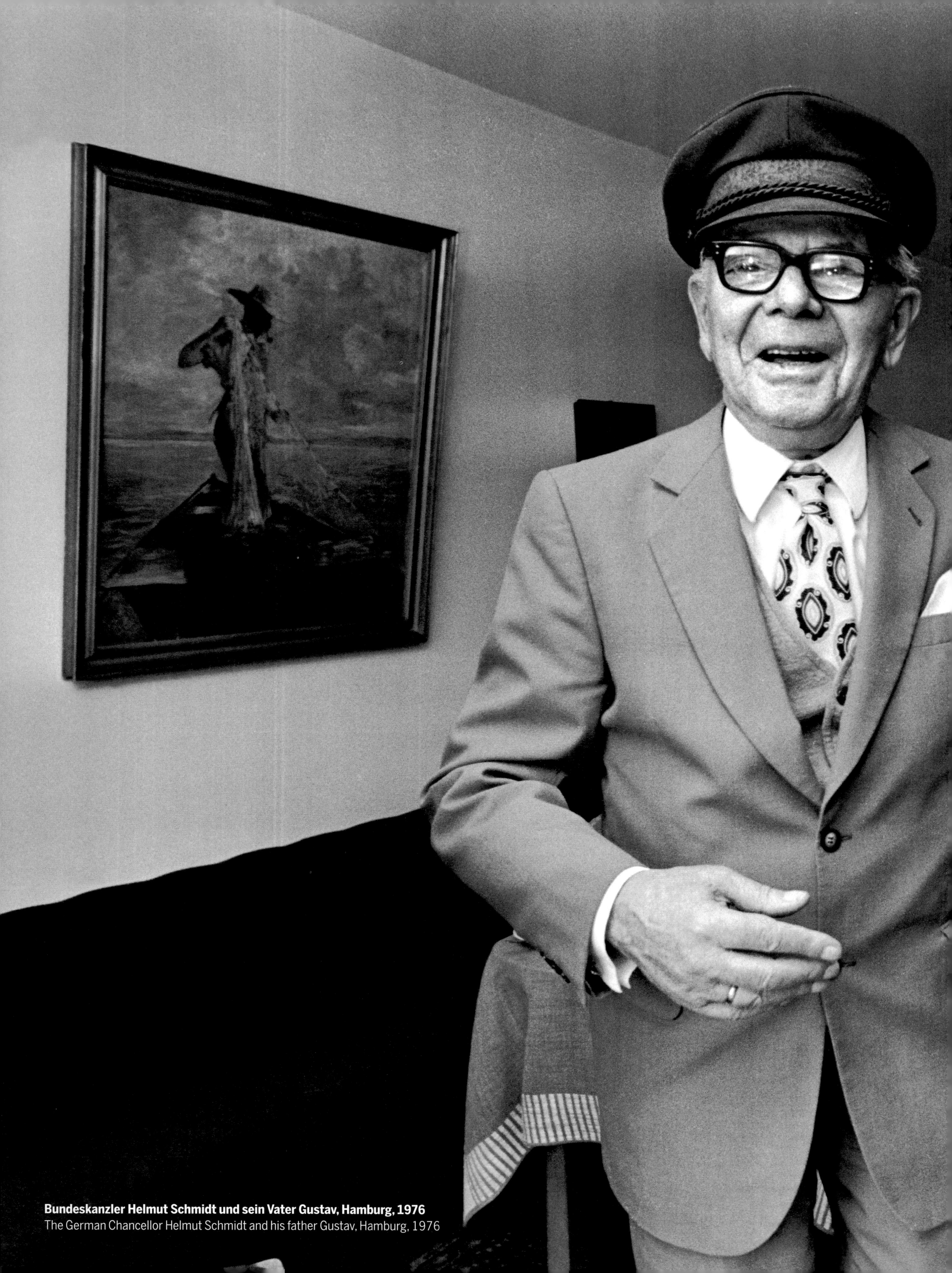

Bundeskanzler Helmut Schmidt und sein Vater Gustav, Hamburg, 1976
The German Chancellor Helmut Schmidt and his father Gustav, Hamburg, 1976

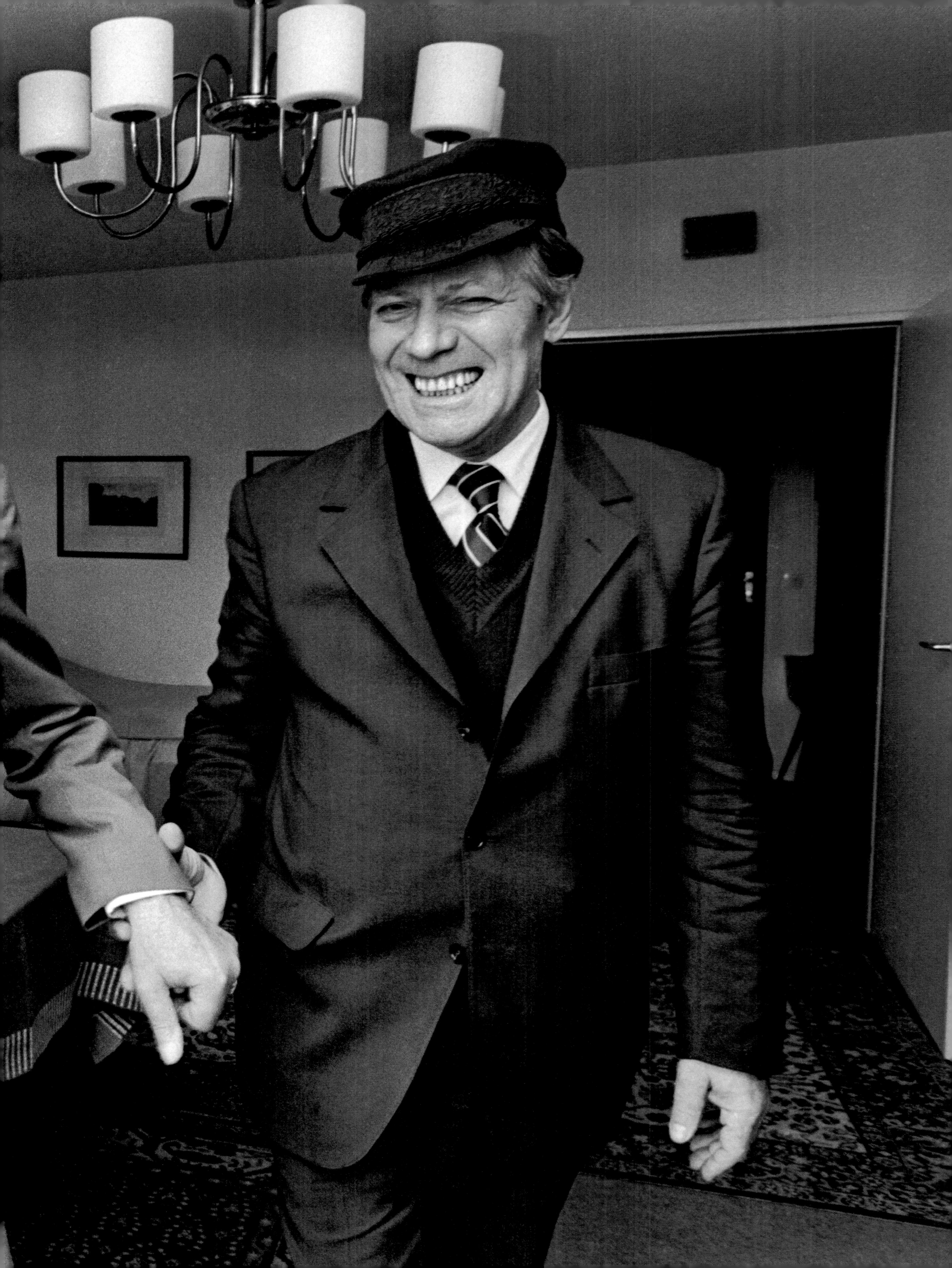

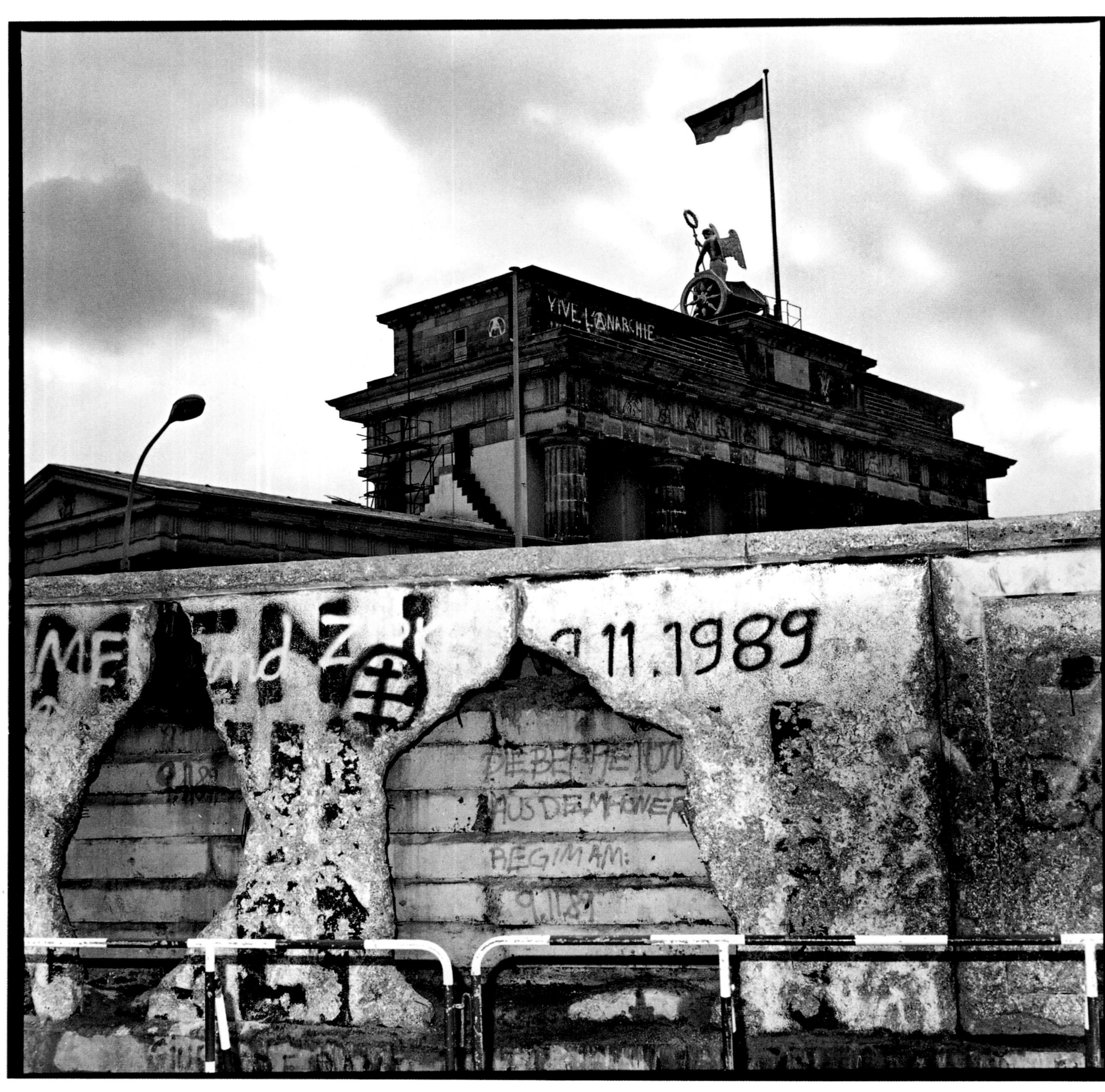

Brandenburger Tor mit Resten der Mauer, Berlin, 1989
The Brandenburg Gate with the remains of the Berlin Wall, Berlin, 1989

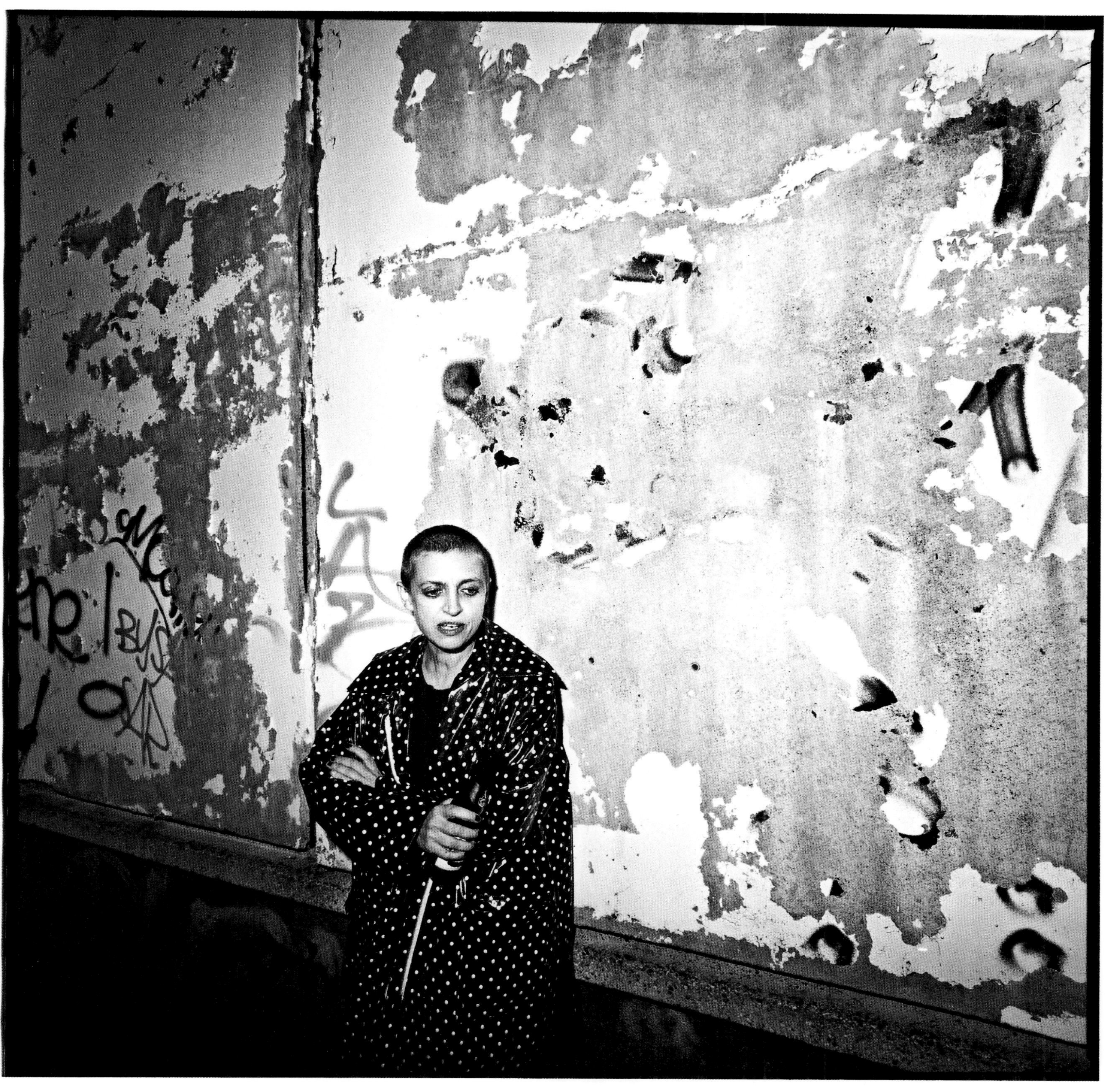

Schauspielerin Katharina Thalbach, Berlin, 1999
The actress Katharina Thalbach, Berlin, 1999

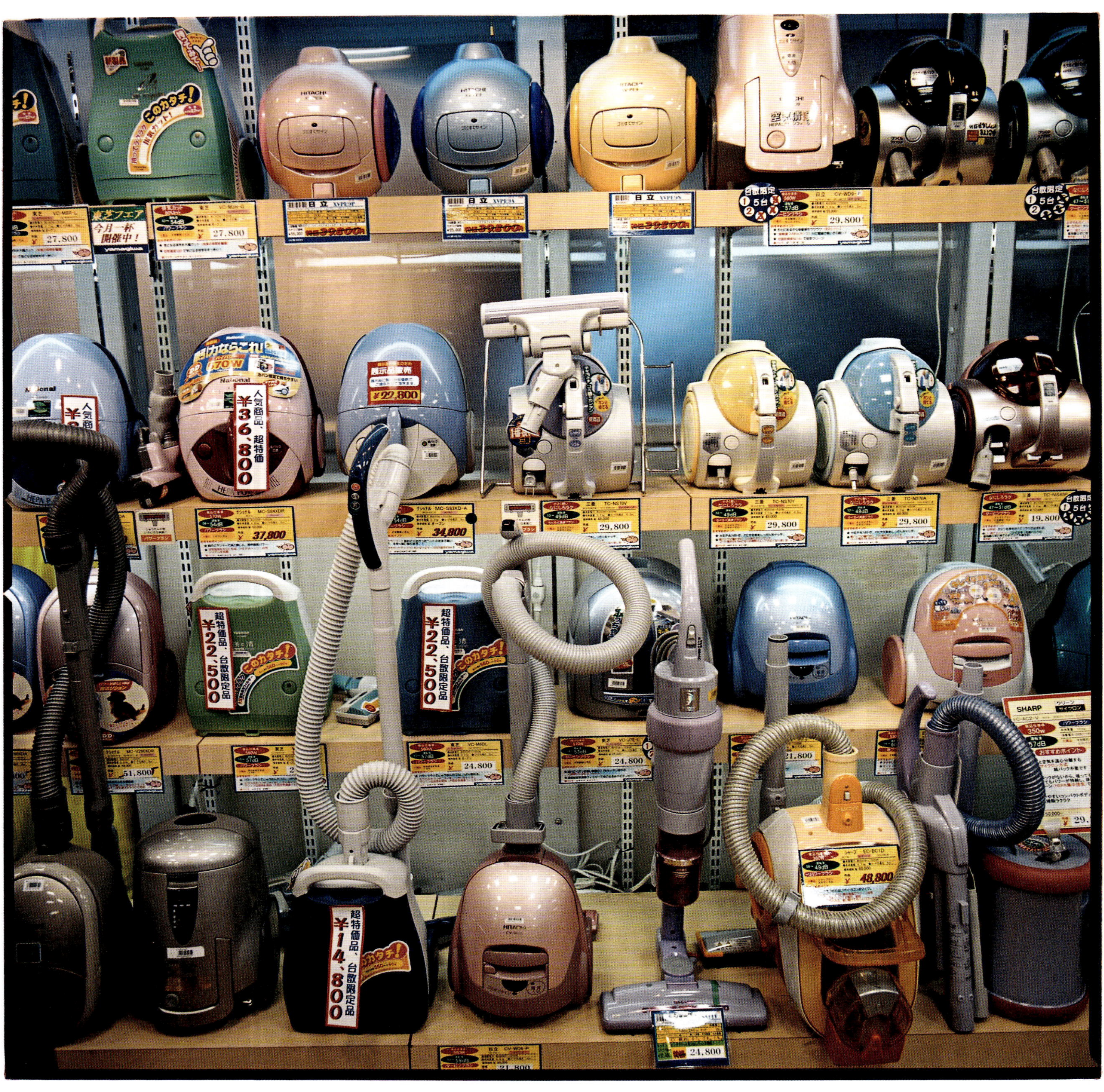

Staubsauger, Tokio, Japan, 2001
Vacuum cleaners, Tokyo, Japan, 2001

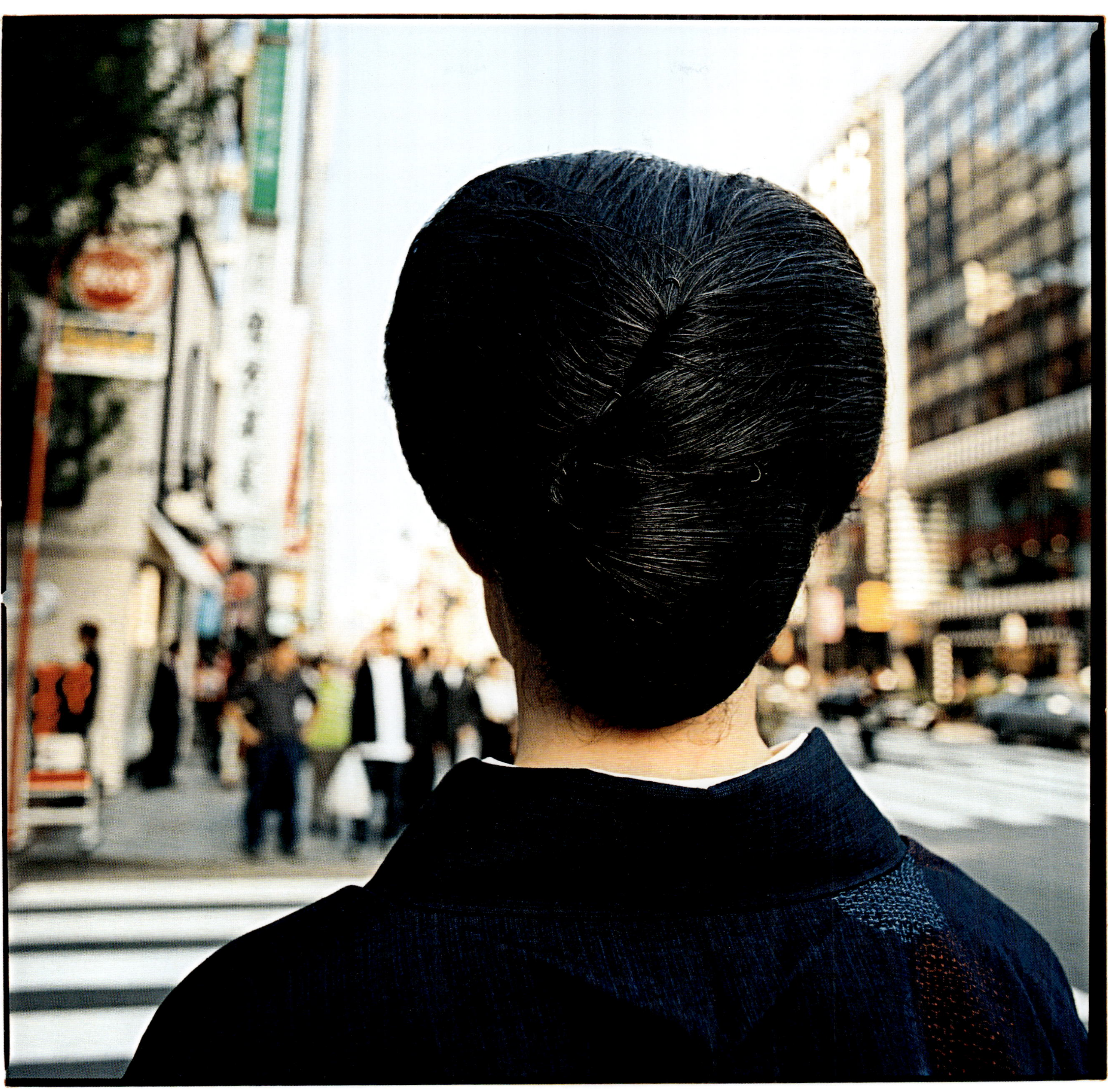

Tokio, Japan, 2001
Tokyo, Japan, 2001

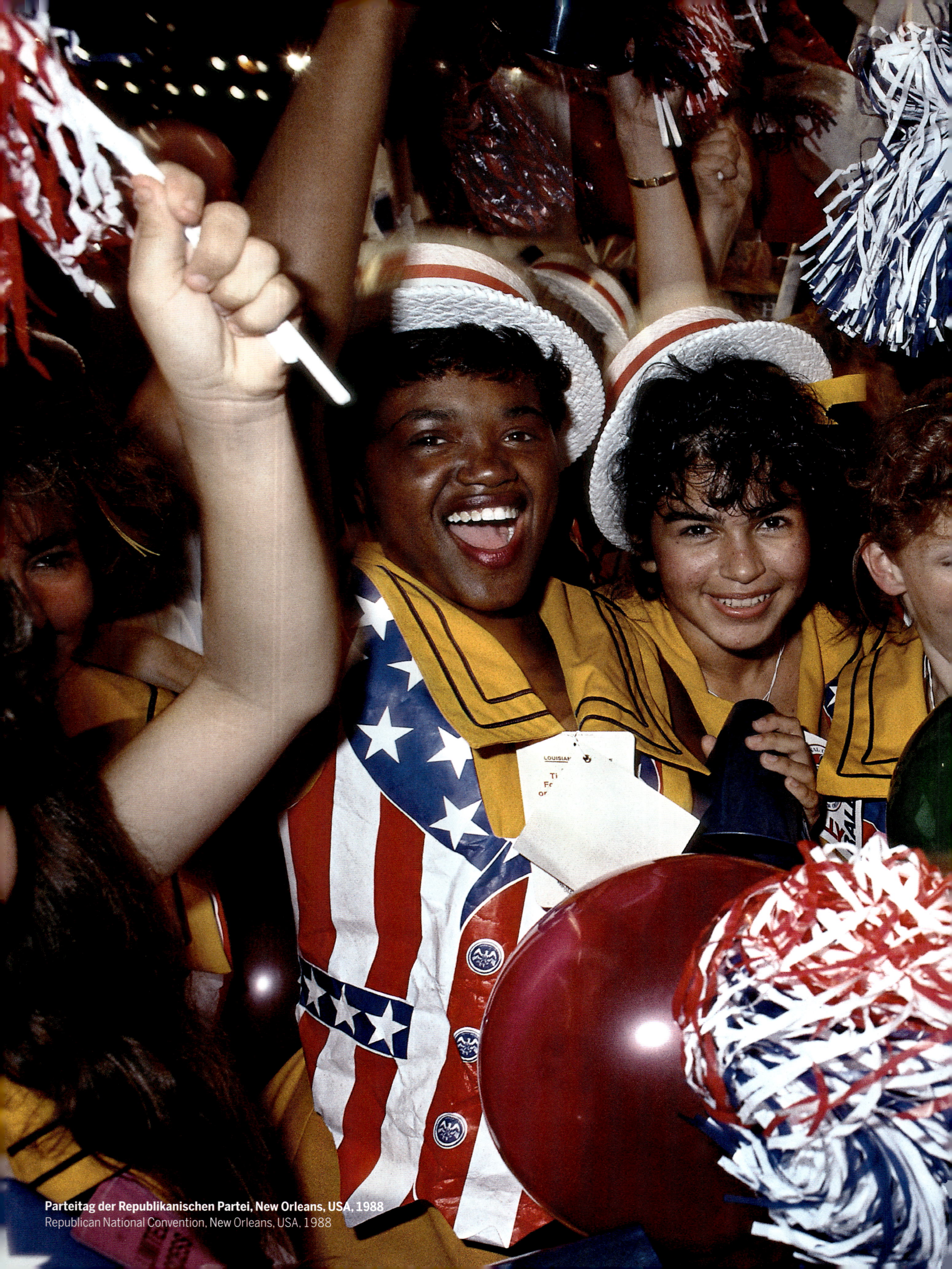

Parteitag der Republikanischen Partei, New Orleans, USA, 1988
Republican National Convention, New Orleans, USA, 1988

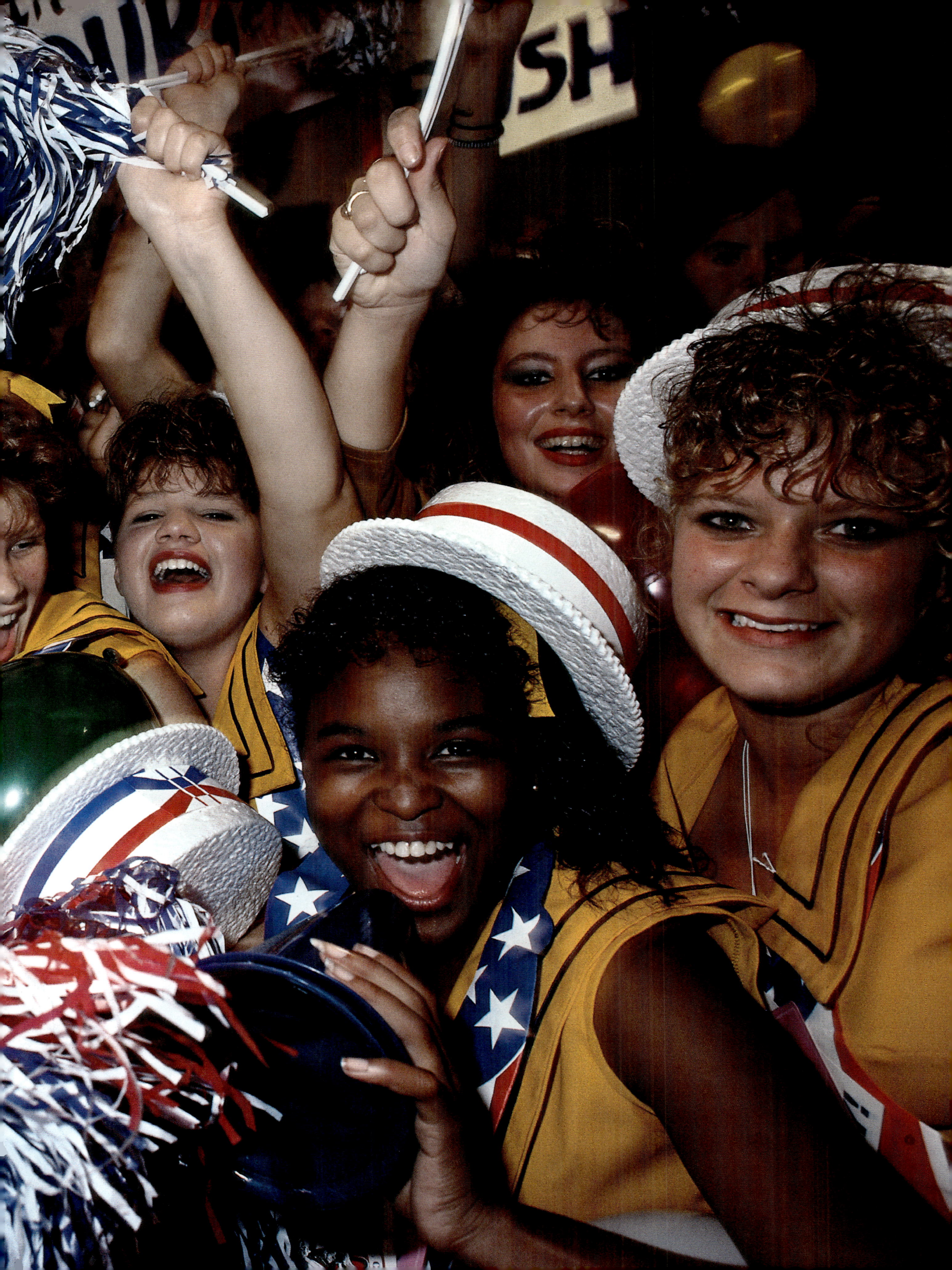

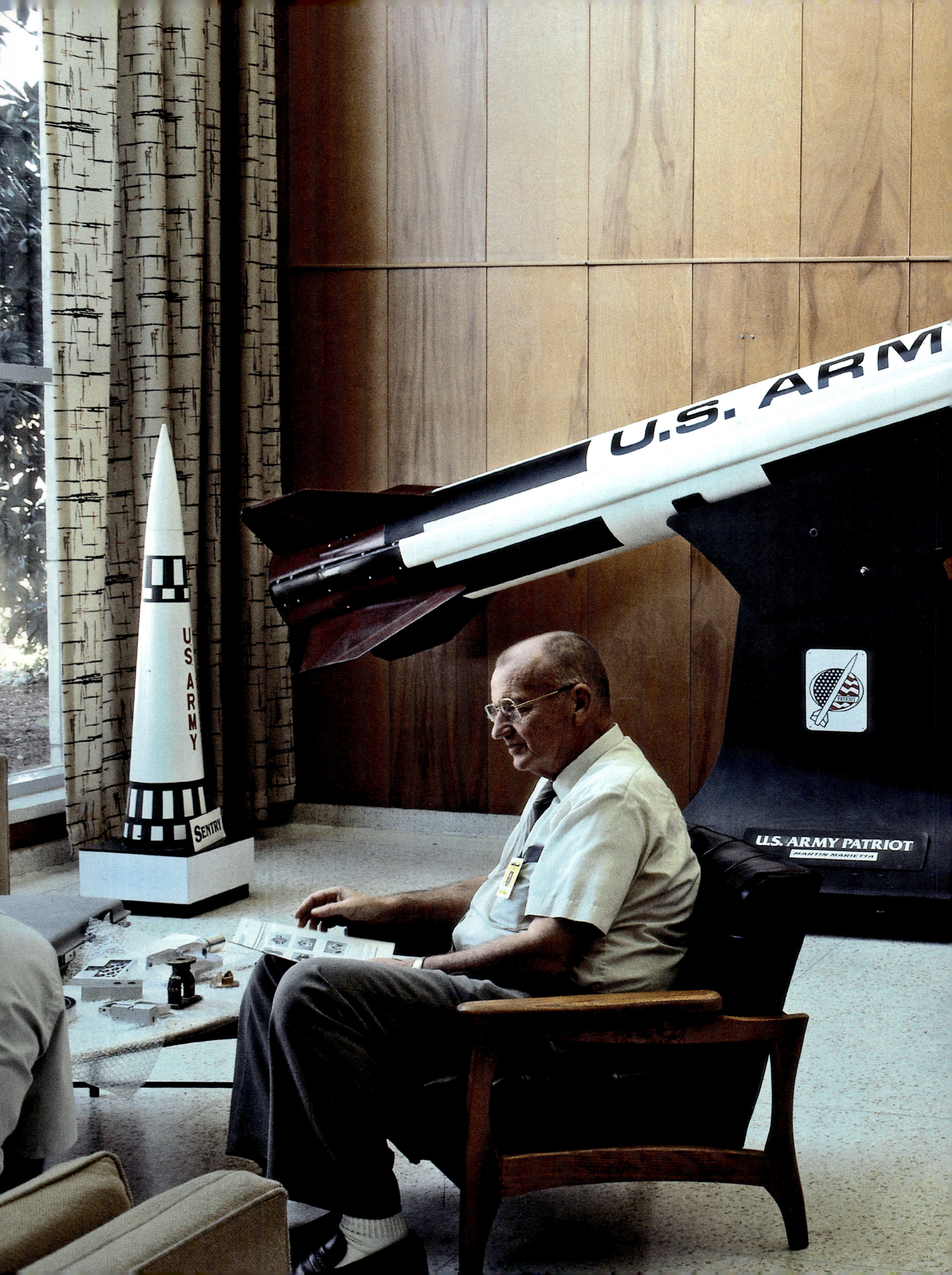
SENTRY
U.S. ARMY
U.S. ARM
U.S. ARMY PATRIOT
MARTIN MARIETTA
PATRIOT

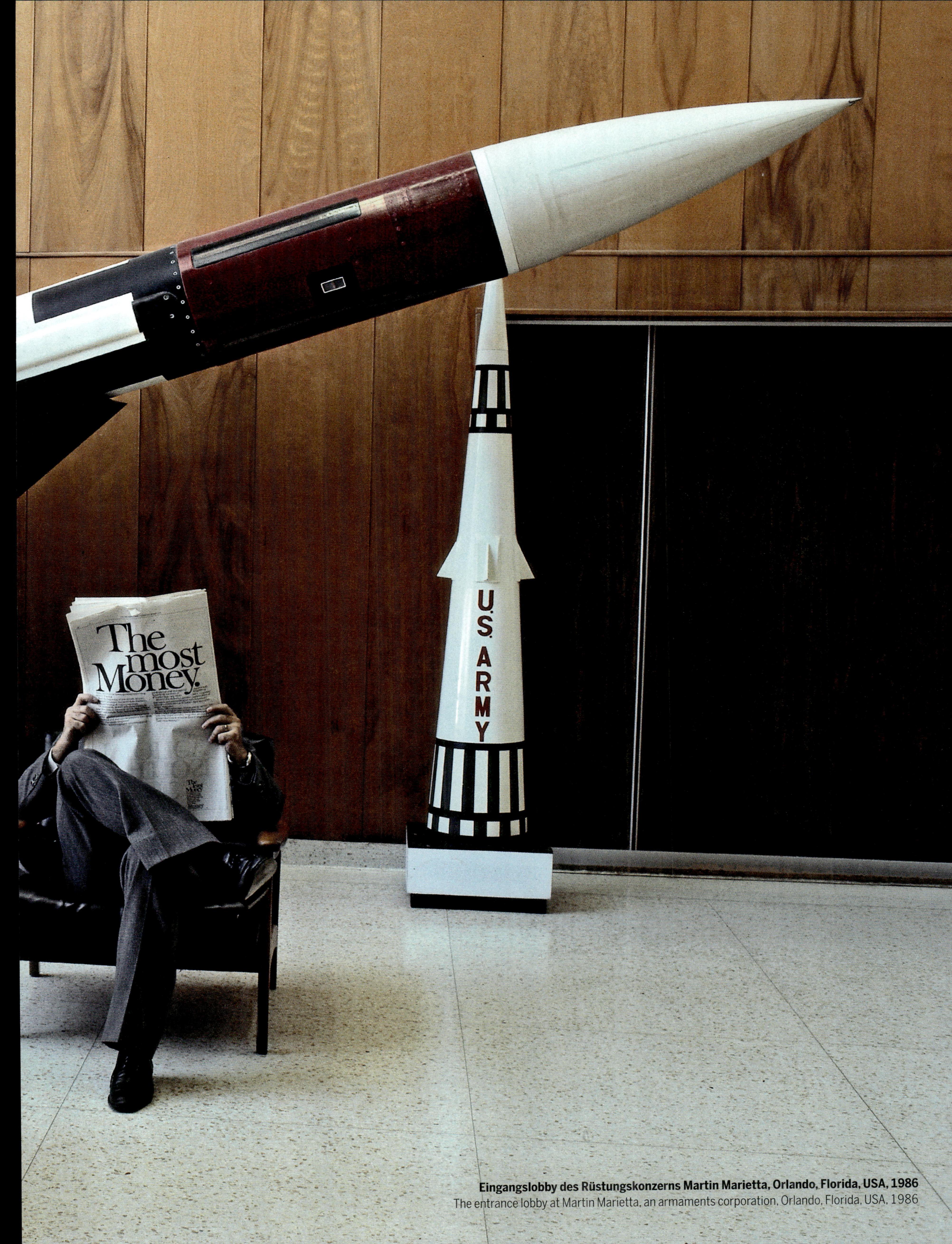

Eingangslobby des Rüstungskonzerns Martin Marietta, Orlando, Florida, USA, 1986
The entrance lobby at Martin Marietta, an armaments corporation, Orlando, Florida, USA, 1986

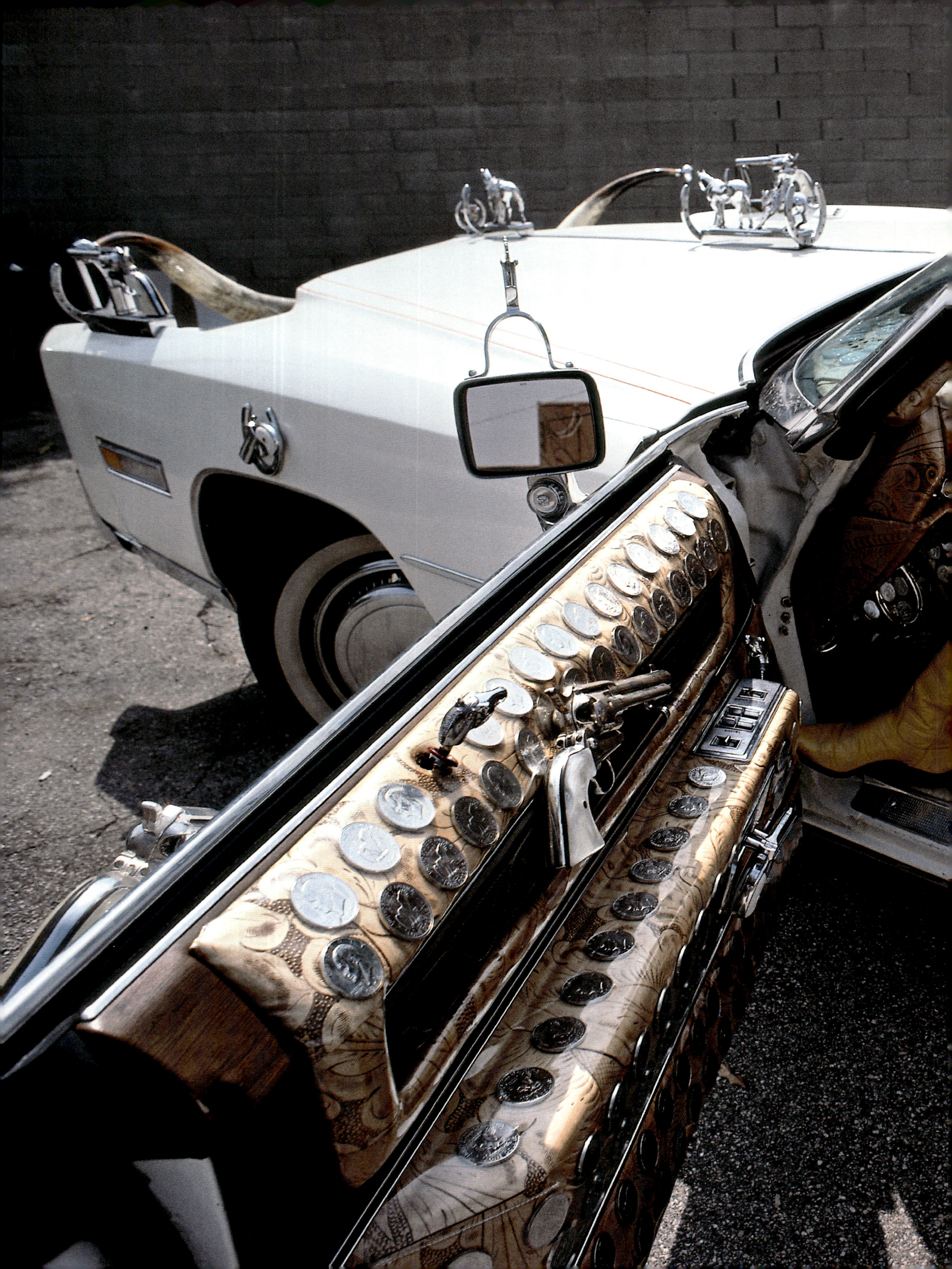

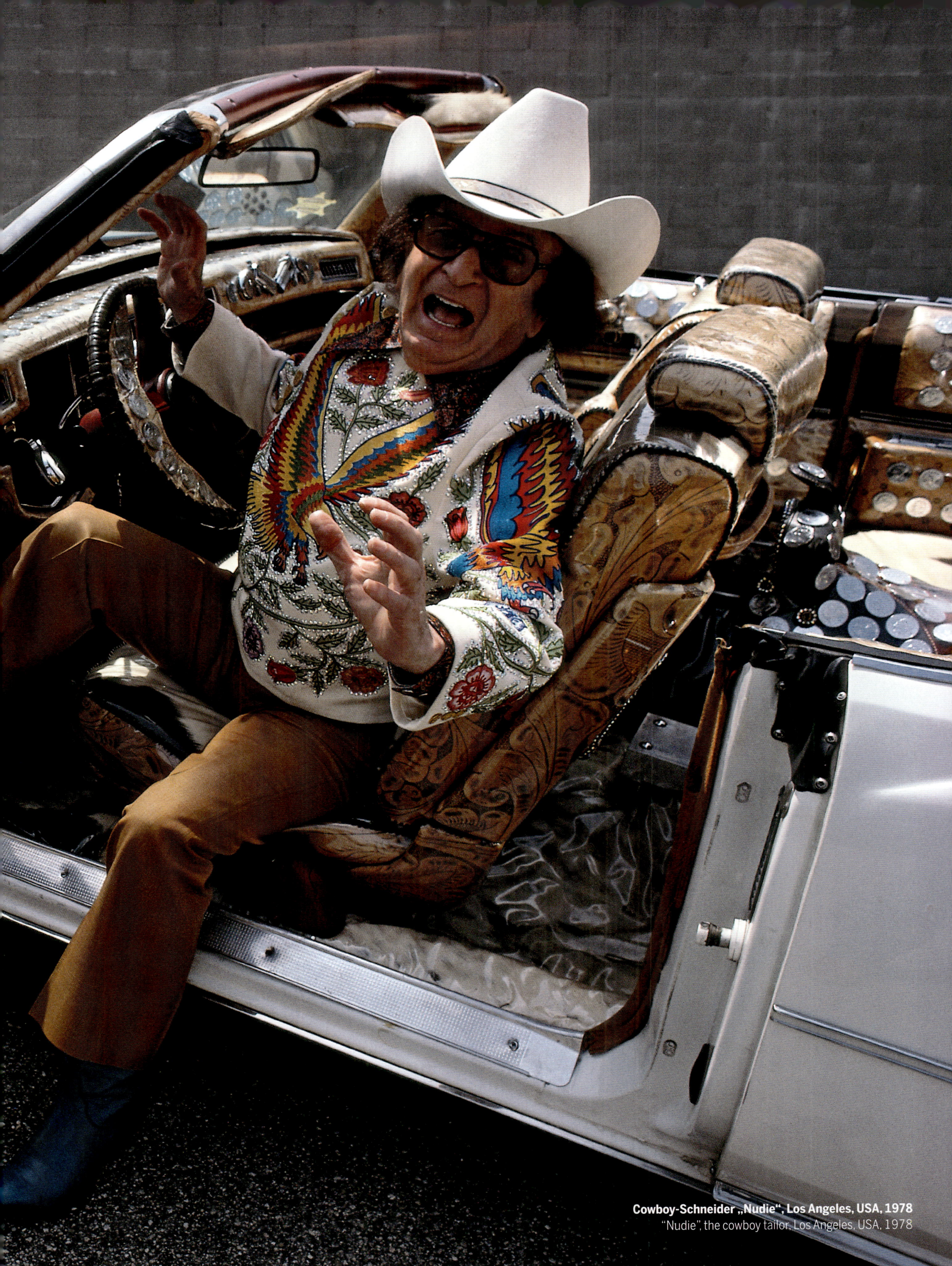

Cowboy-Schneider „Nudie", Los Angeles, USA, 1978
"Nudie", the cowboy tailor, Los Angeles, USA, 1978

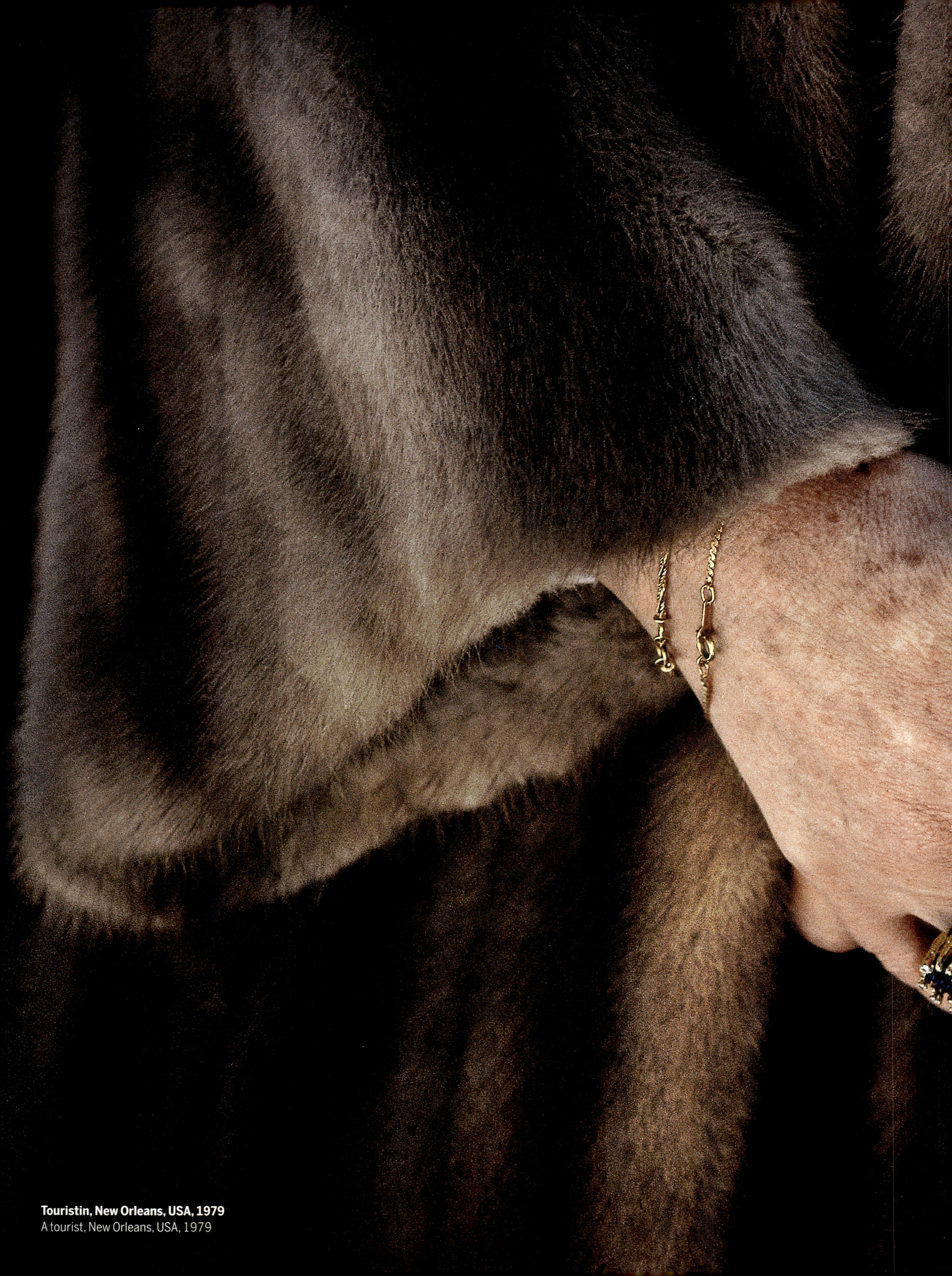

Touristin, New Orleans, USA, 1979
A tourist, New Orleans, USA, 1979

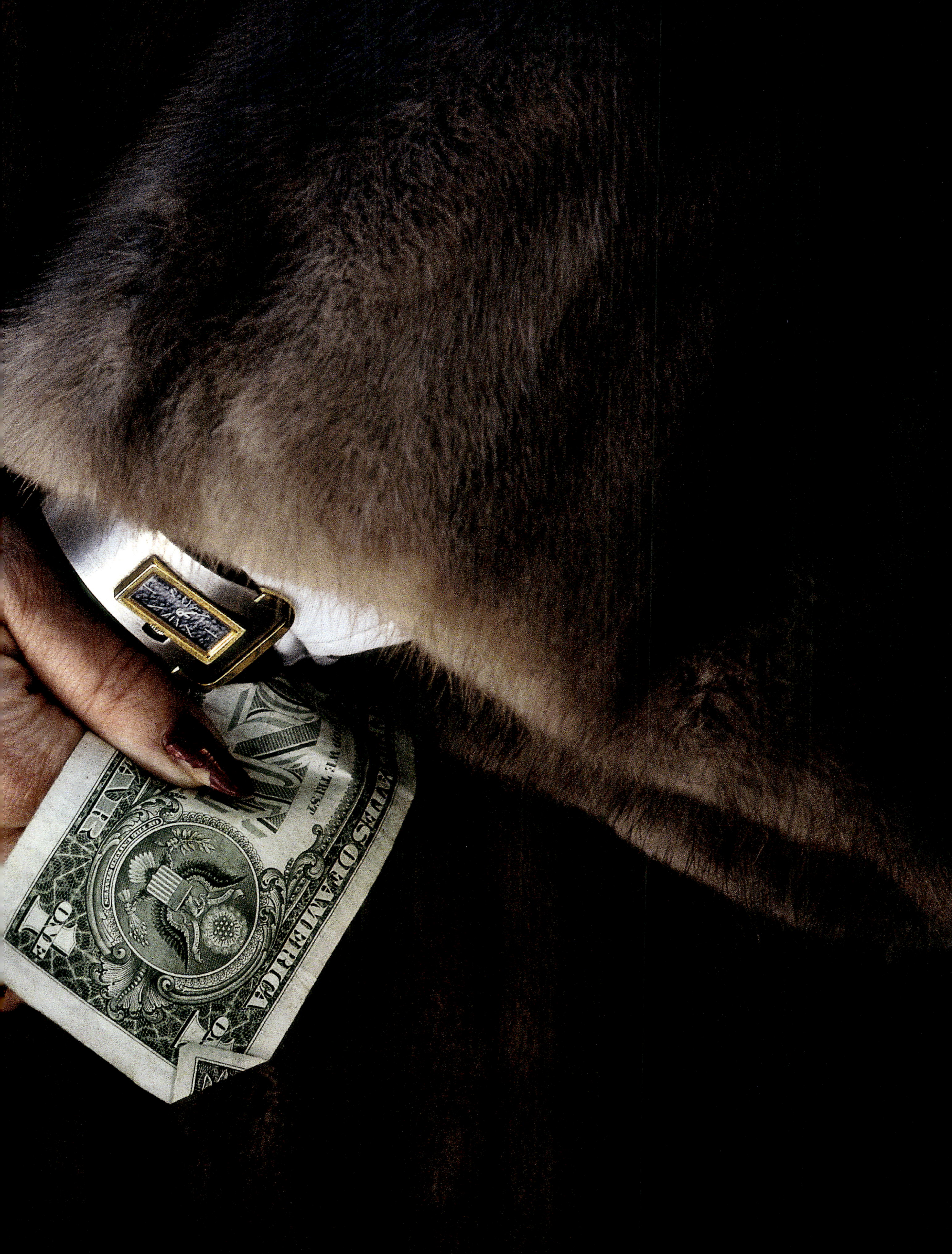

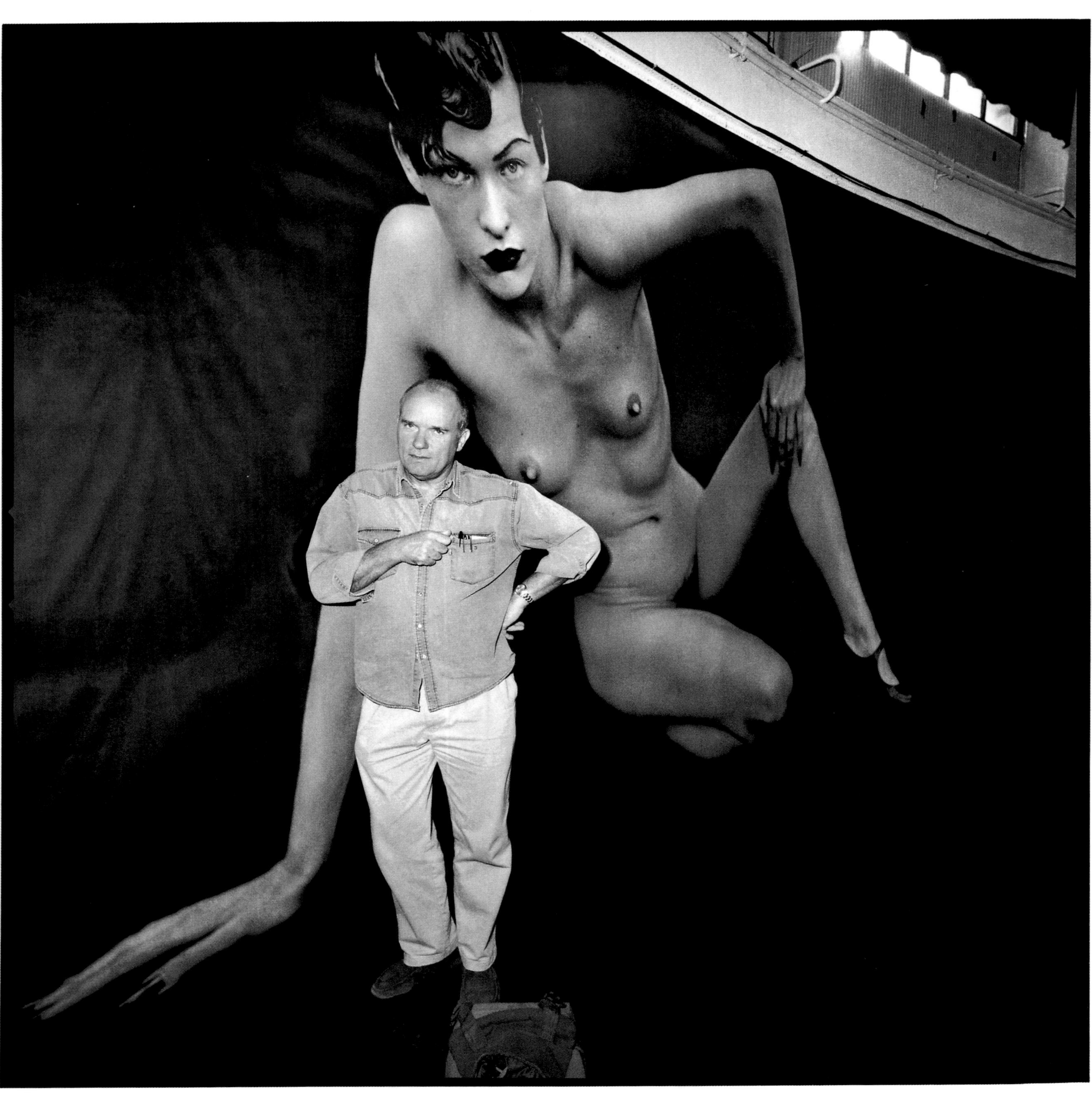

Fotograf Peter Lindbergh, Mailand, 1998
The photographer Peter Lindbergh, Milan, 1998

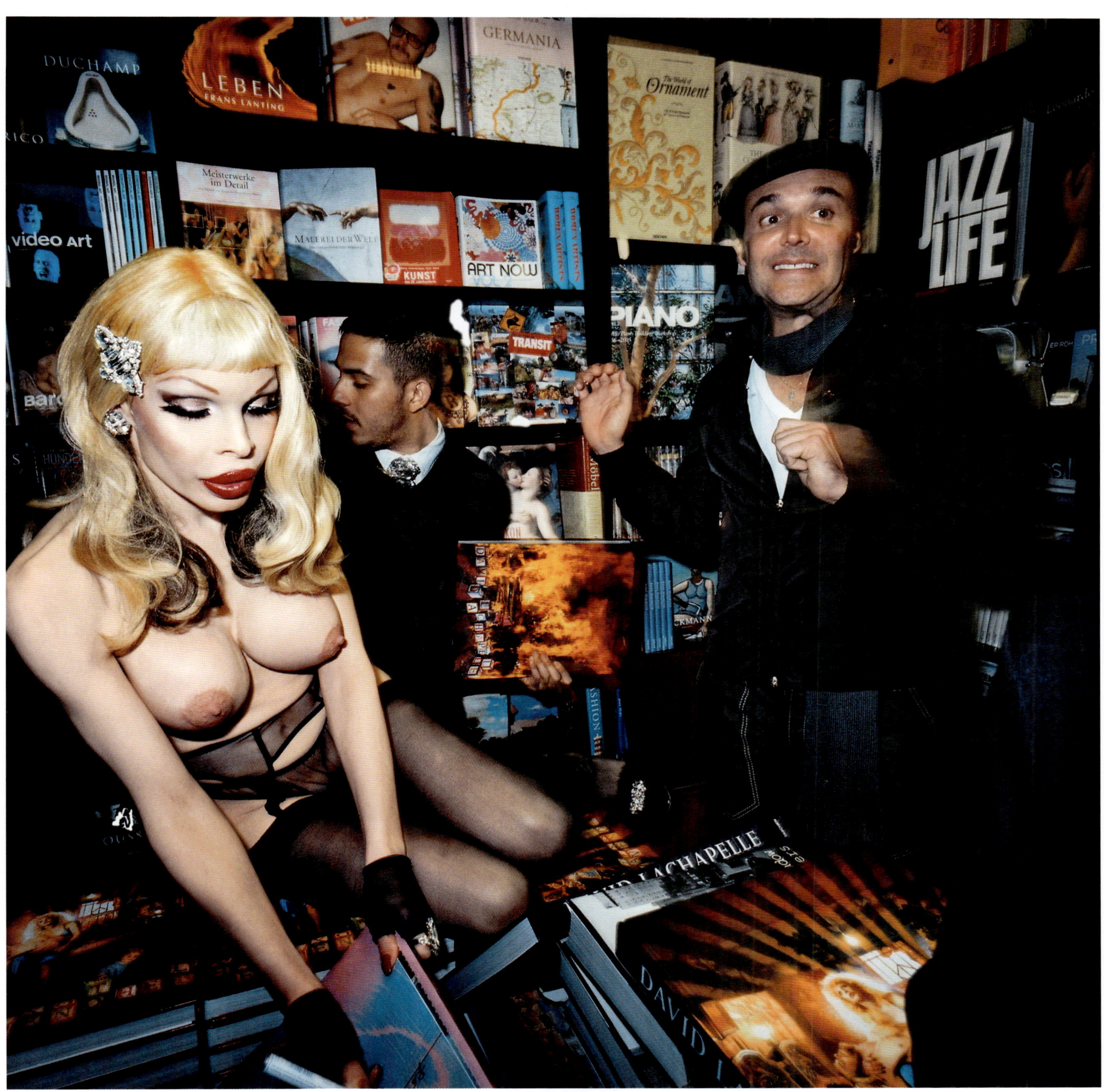

Fotograf David LaChapelle und seine Muse Amanda Lepore, Berlin, 2005
The photographer David LaChapelle and his muse Amanda Lepore, Berlin, 2005

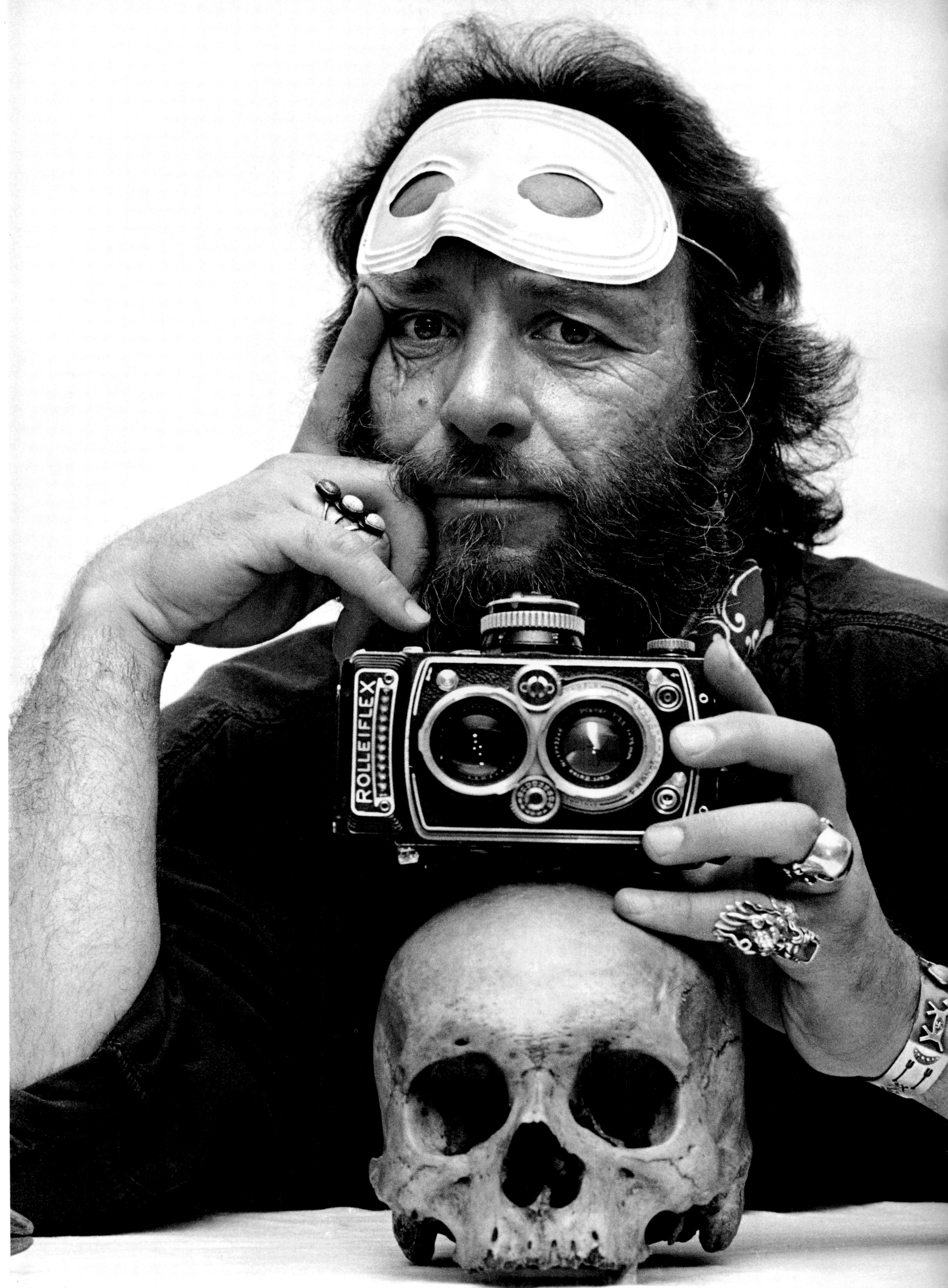

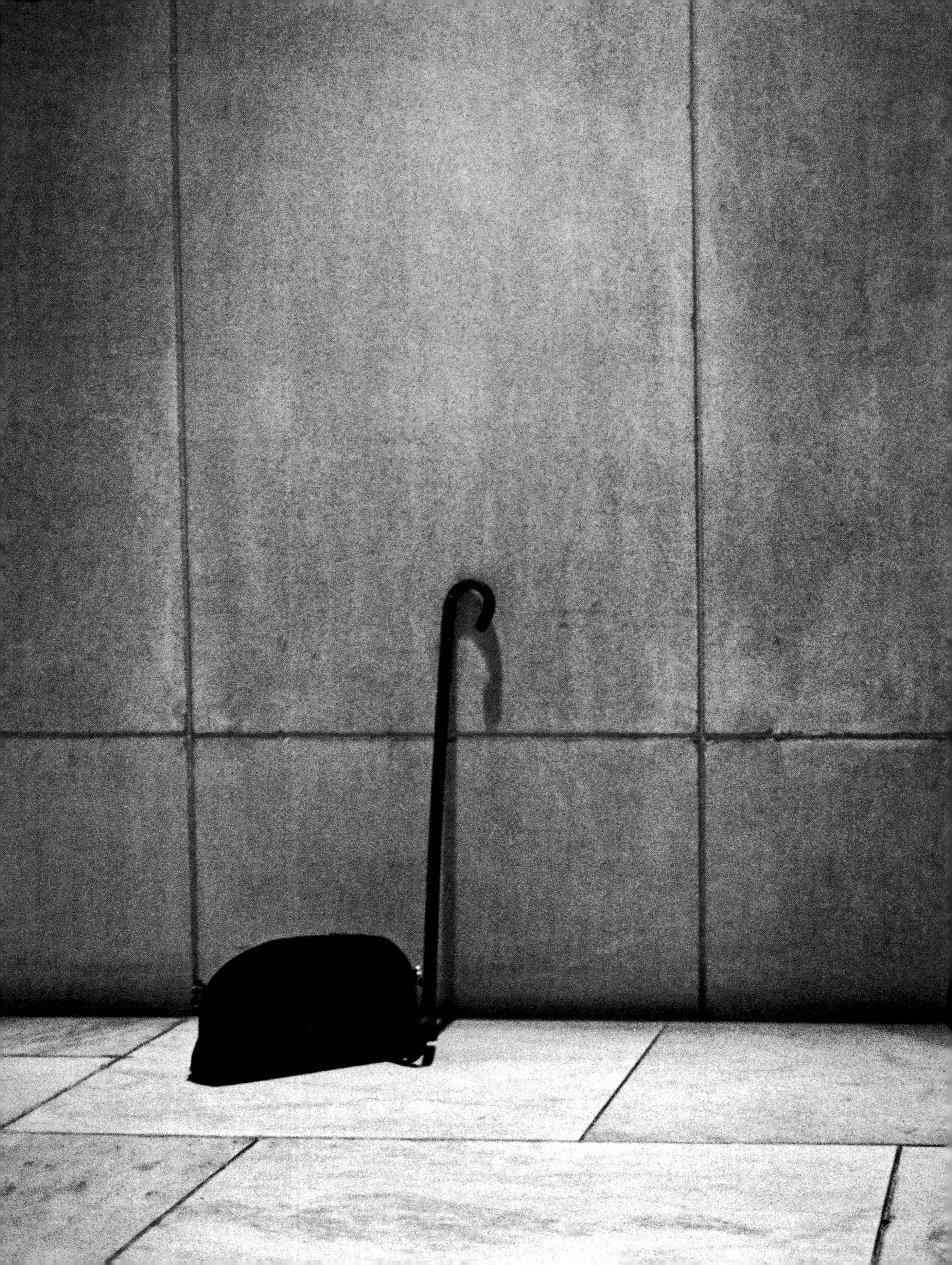

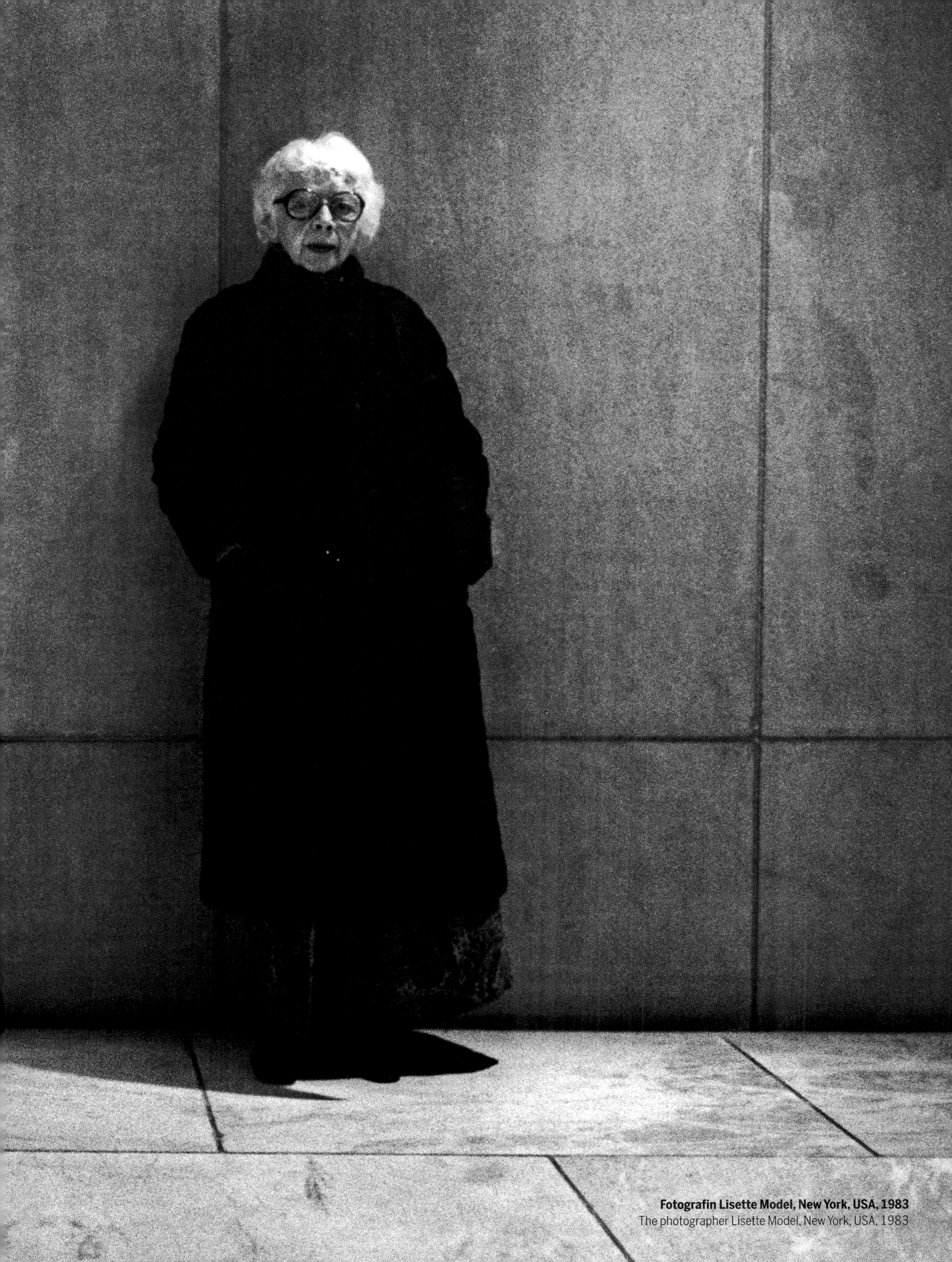

Fotografin Lisette Model, New York, USA, 1983
The photographer Lisette Model, New York, USA, 1983

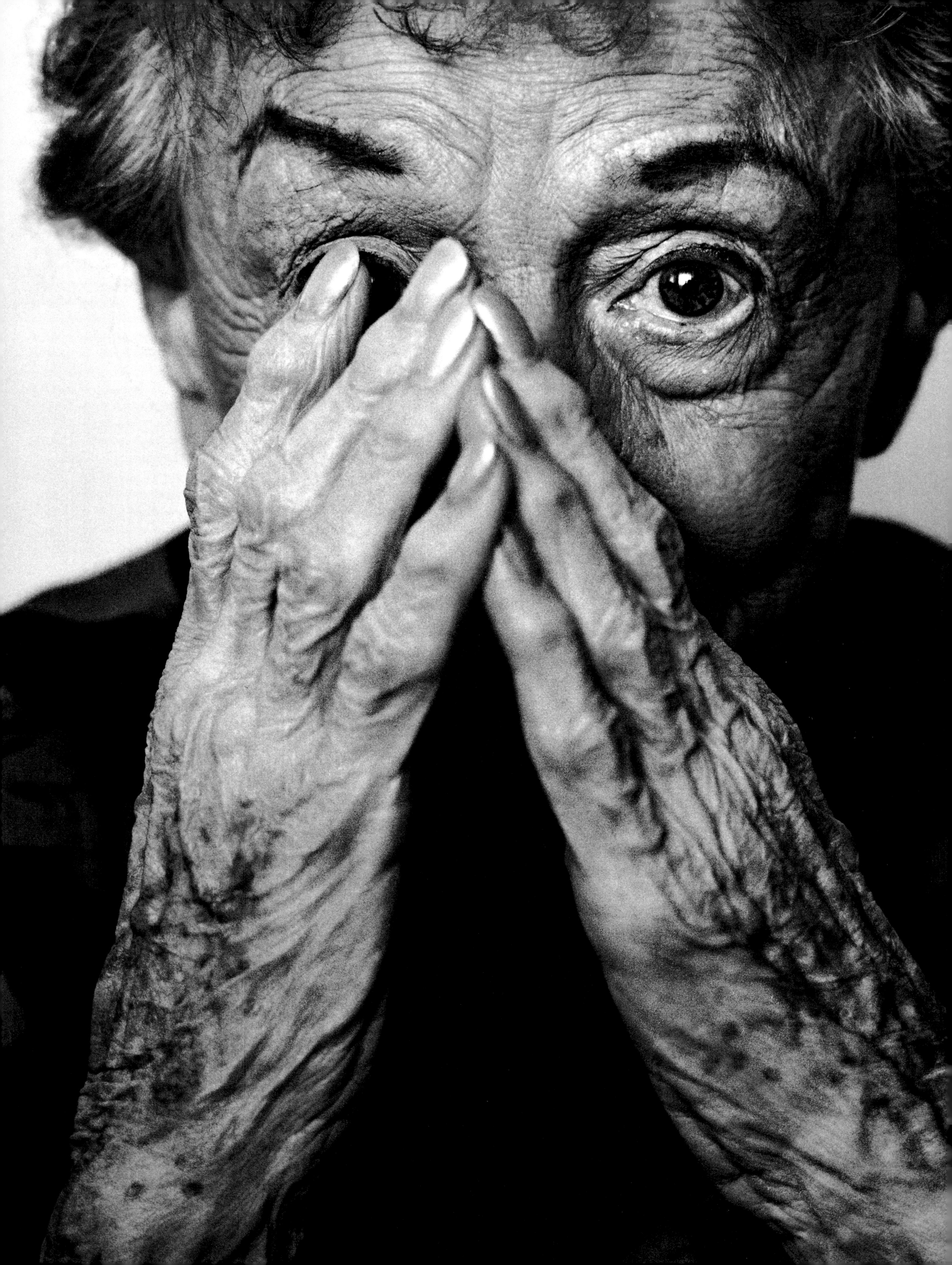

Fotografin Ruth Bernhard, San Francisco, USA, 2000
The photographer Ruth Bernhard, San Francisco, USA, 2000

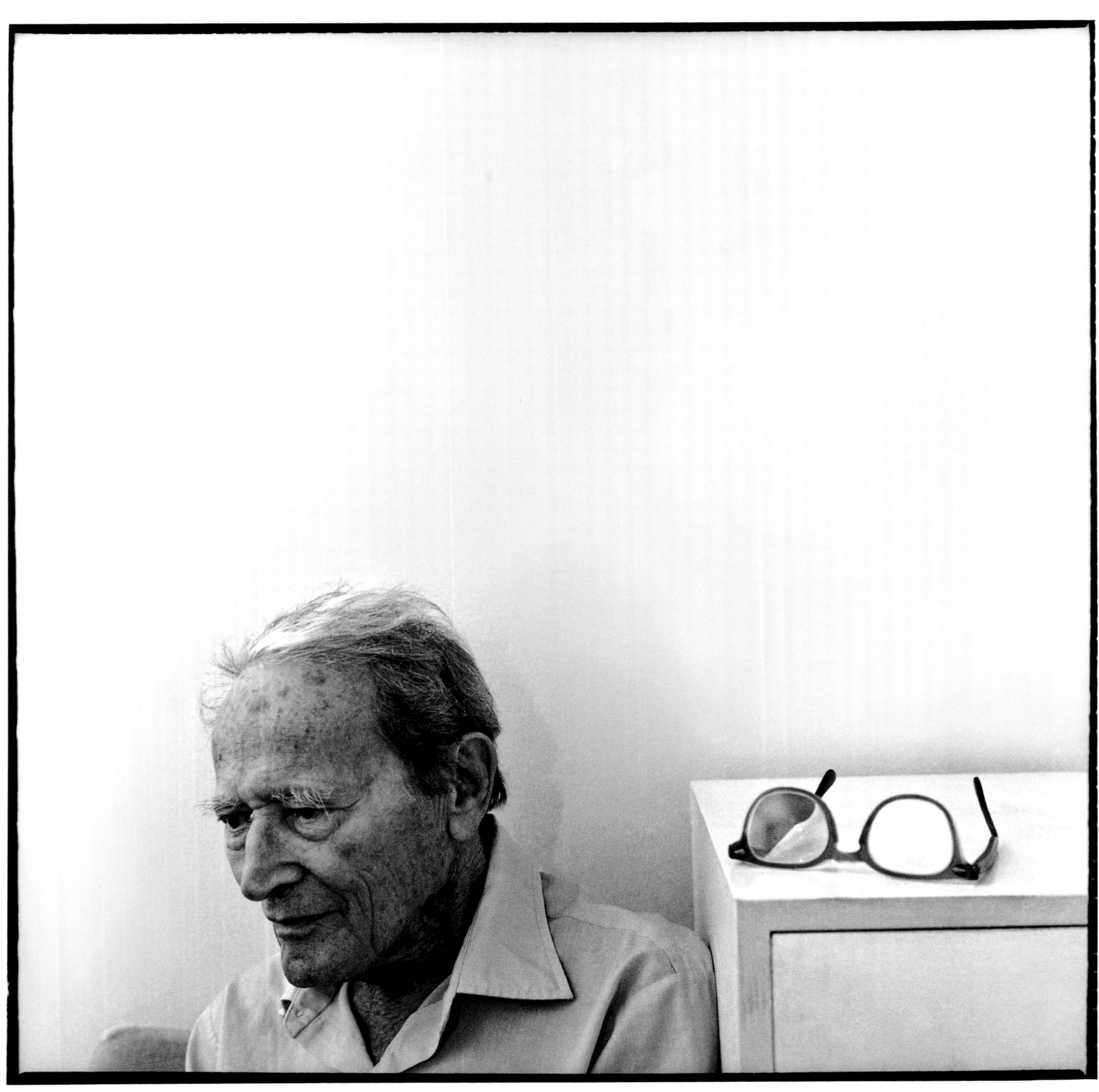

Fotograf Andreas Feininger, New York, USA, 1996
The photographer Andreas Feininger, New York, USA, 1996

Fotograf Helmut Newton mit seiner Frau June, Monte Carlo, 1983
The photographer Helmut Newton and his wife June, Monte Carlo, 1983

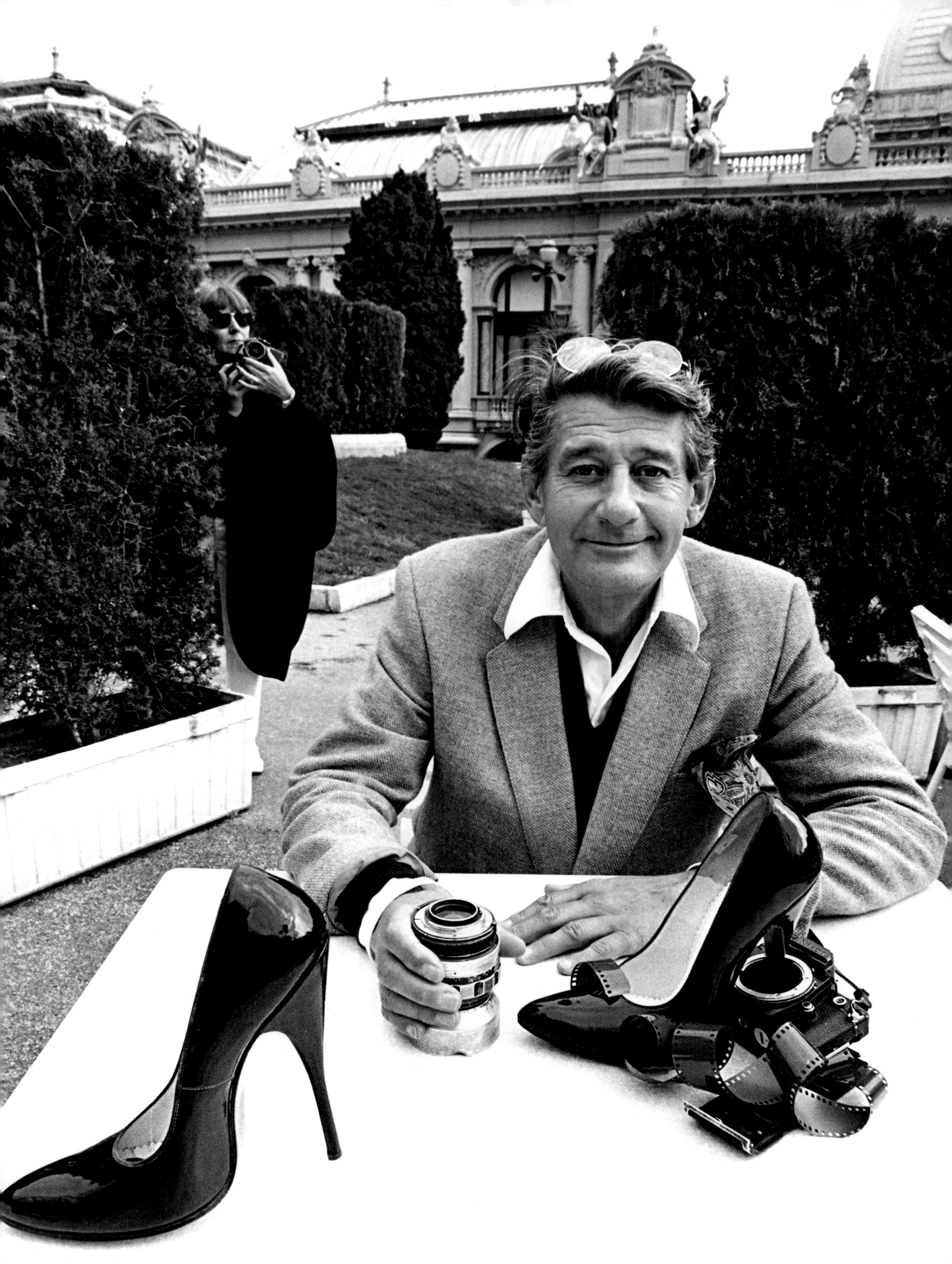

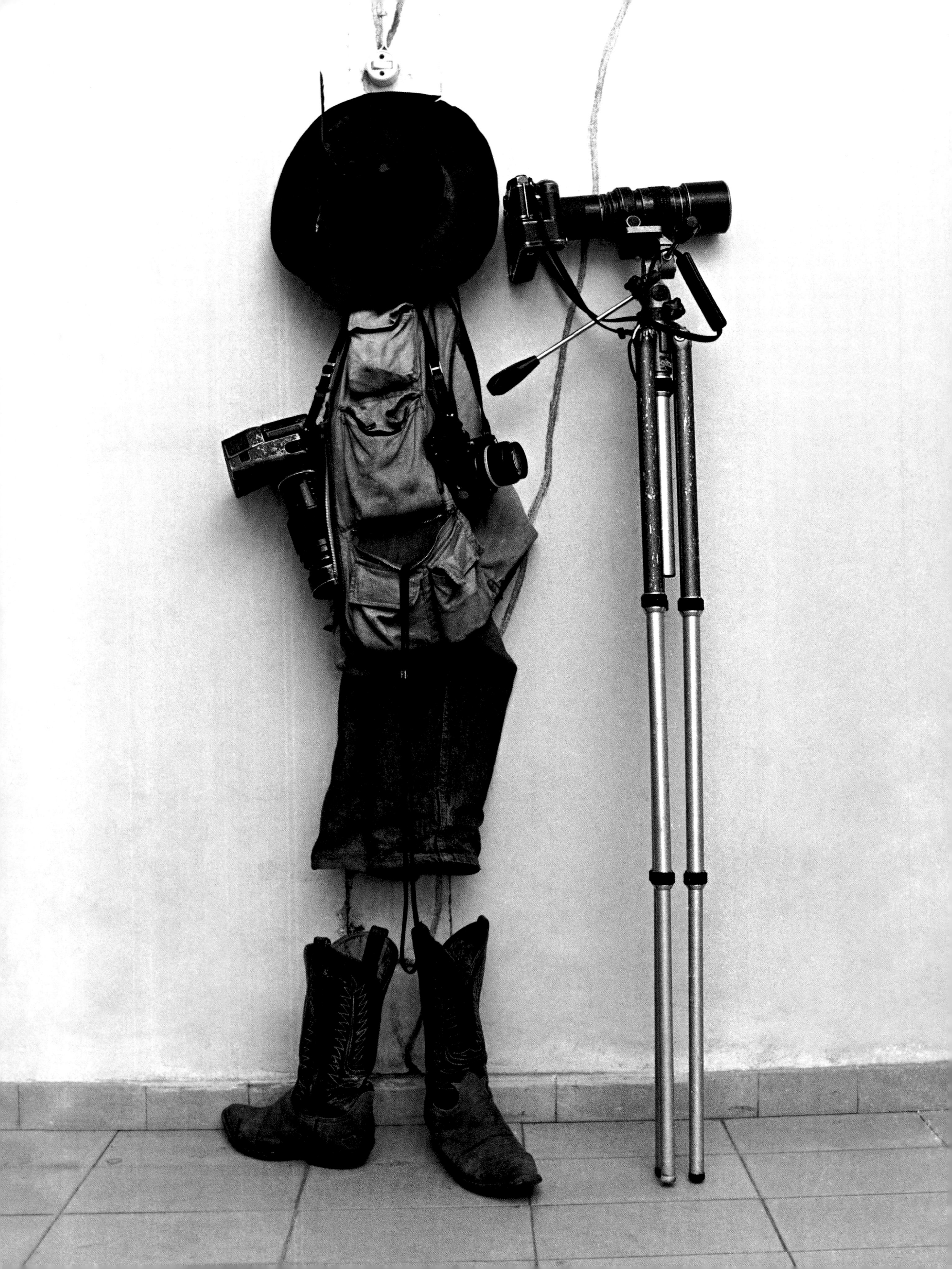

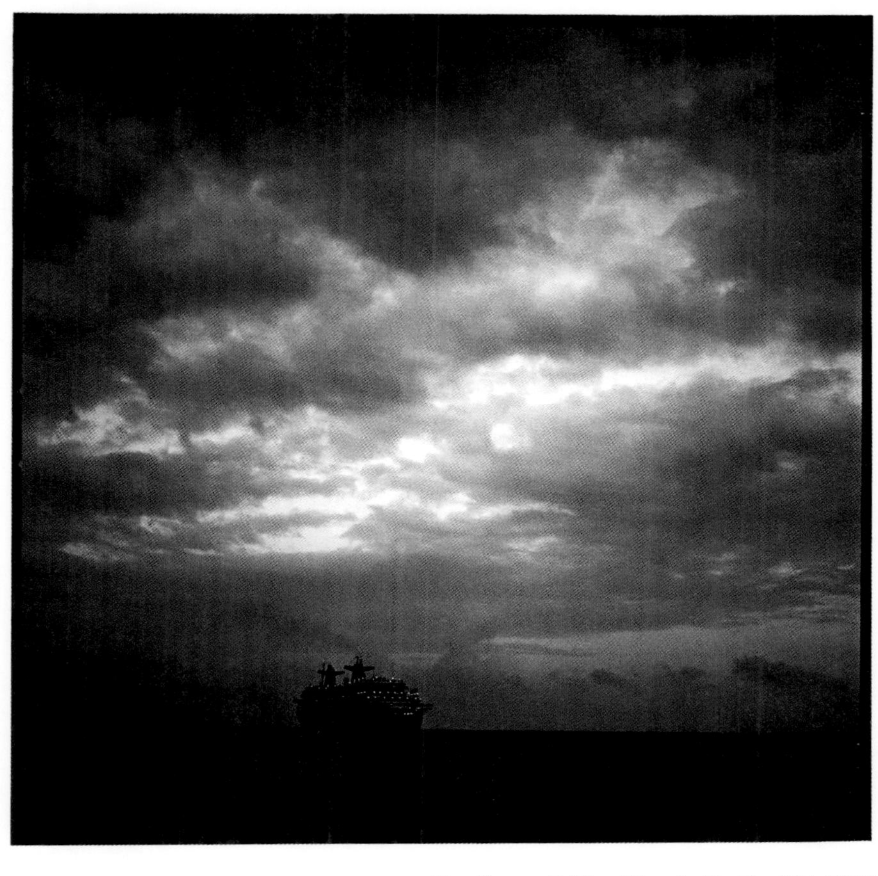

Die „Norway", Miami Beach, Florida, USA, 2000
The *Norway*, Miami Beach, Florida, USA, 2000

Mein Stillleben, Pantanal, Brasilien, 1987
My still life, Pantanal, Brazil, 1987

munch.
macke.
miró.

-50%*

*Wenn Sie das Kunstmagazin art abonnieren, bekommen Sie gratis die artcard dazu – und sparen damit bei bedeutenden Museen bis zu 50% Eintritt.

Sie verpassen also keine Ausgabe mehr und erleben über 100 Museen in Deutschland, Österreich und der Schweiz exklusiv zum artcard-Tarif. Mehr Informationen unter **www.art-magazin.de/artcard** oder direkt abonnieren unter **01805 - 86180 00** (14 Cent/Min. aus dem dt. Festnetz, max. 42 Cent/Min. aus dem dt. Mobilfunknetz)

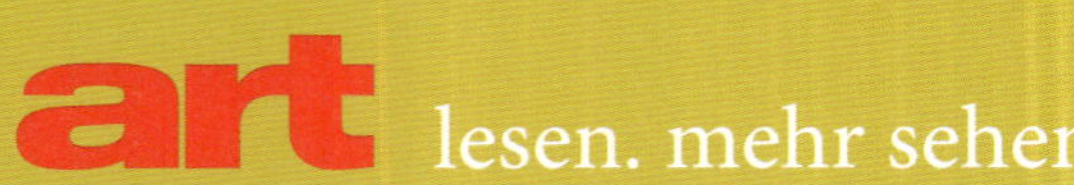

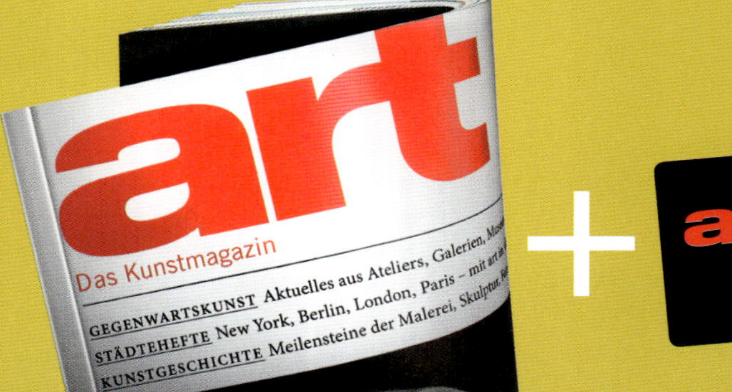

Babelsberg

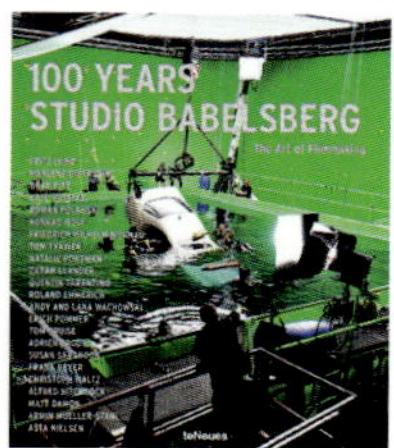

Seit 100 Jahren die Fabrik der laufenden Bilder – große deutsche Filme wurden hier gedreht, Hollywood produziert hier, Weltstars lieben das Studio. Eine großartige Bilderreise vom Stummfilm bis heute vor und hinter den Kulissen unseres Vorstadt-Hollywoods.

A century of moving pictures from a great German film factory: Hollywood produces here, international stars love the studios. From silent movies to the present day, backdrops and backstage – a magnificent pictorial journey through Berlin's "Hollywood suburb".

100 Years Studio Babelsberg,
teNeues, 59,90 Euro

Ritts

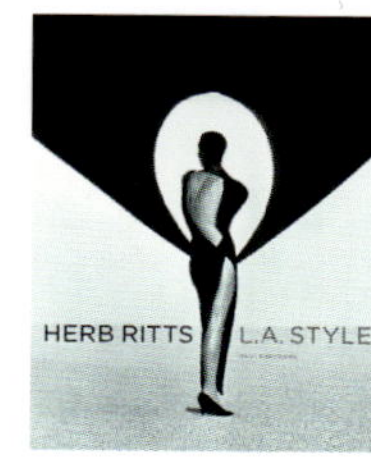

Er war der fotografische Bildhauer der 80er und 90er Jahre, seine Bilder waren die Neuformulierung einer Körpersprache und eines Starkultes. Dieser Band zeigt die wichtigsten wie auch bislang unveröffentlichte Werke des 2002 verstorbenen Herb Ritts.

Herb Ritts, who died in 2002, was the photographic sculptor of the 1980s and 1990s. His pictures were a restatement of body language and star cult. This album presents us with his most important and many hitherto unpublished photos.

Herb Ritts, L.A. Style,
Schirmer/Mosel, 78 Euro

Drtikol

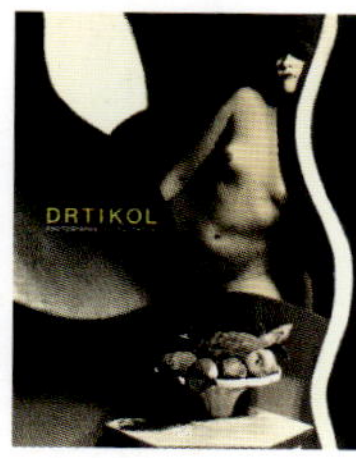

Fast vergessen und nun wiederentdeckt sind die Aktfotografien des Tschechen František Drtikol. Eine Schatzkammer künstlerischer, vom Expressionismus und Kubismus geprägter Fotografie, in der Frauen mal als Nymphe, mal als Femme fatale erscheinen.

Long forgotten and now rediscovered, the Czech photographer František Drtikol's nude photos are a treasure chamber of artistic, expressionist- and cubist-like photography where women appear as anything from nymphs to femme fatales.

František Drtikol, Photographie,
Hatje Cantz, 35 Euro

Galella

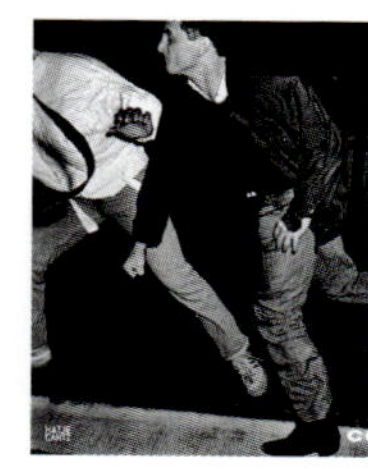

Die Bilder des legendären Paparazzo Ron Galella sind rau und schnell, aber auf den zweiten Blick auch anmutig und verehrend. Jacqueline Kennedy hasste ihn, Andy Warhol liebte ihn, und mancher schlug ihn. Und so sind seine Bilder – liebevolle Anschläge.

The photos shot by the legendary paparazzo Ron Galella are raw and fast. But at second glance they are also charming and adoring. Jackie Kennedy hated him, Andy Warhol loved him and others tried to hit him. His photos are like that – affectionate attacks.

Ron Galella, Paparazzo Extraordinaire,
Hatje Cantz, 29,80 Euro

Braschler/Fischer

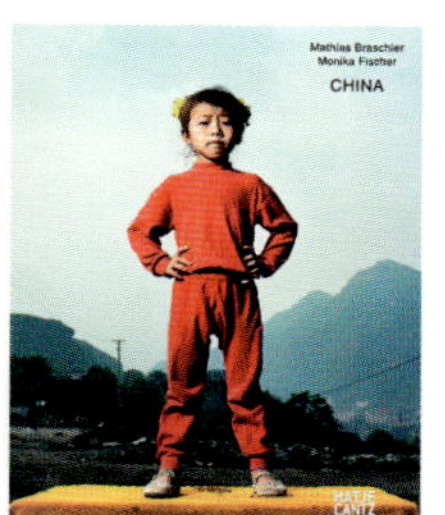

Sie sind 30 000 Kilometer durch China gefahren und haben jeden Tag einen Menschen fotografiert – den armen Bauern, den reichen Yachtclubbesitzer und das Mädchen aus dem Wanderzirkus. Ein beeindruckendes Menschenporträt des Riesenreiches.

They travelled 30,000 km through China and photographed a different person every day: the poor peasant, the rich yacht club owner, the girl from the travelling circus – an impressive portfolio of portraits from this huge country.

Braschler/Fischer, China,
Hatje Cantz, 39,80 Euro

McKell

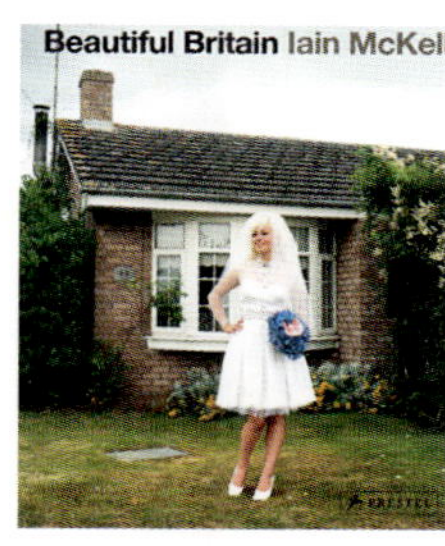

Seit über 30 Jahren schaut der Fotograf McKell seinem Volk zu, den Briten. Und so sind seine Bilder: ein Land aus Teetrinkern, Bankenzockern, Punks, Dicken am Strand von Brighton und dämmernden Ruinen einer alten Industrie. Sehr britisch schön.

For more than 30 years, McKell has been observing his British compatriots. And his photos show us a country of tea drinkers, financial sharks, punks, fatties on Brighton beach and the crumbling ruins of an industrial past. Very British.

Iain McKell, Beautiful Britain,
Prestel, 29,95 Euro

State of the Art

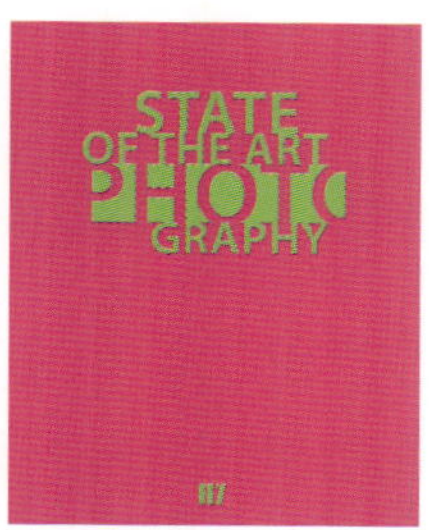

Wer fotografiert eigentlich zurzeit warum und was? Dieser Band zeigt einen aktuellen Überblick über den Zustand der jungen Fotografie heute. Auffällig, wie intensiv sich die Fotografie den Themen der Zeit wie Migration und Globalisierung stellt.

Who photographs what, and why? This album shows us the state of the art in young photography today. What you notice is how intensively these photographers confront contemporary topics such as migration or globalisation.

State of the Art Photography,
Feymedia, 35 Euro

Willoughby

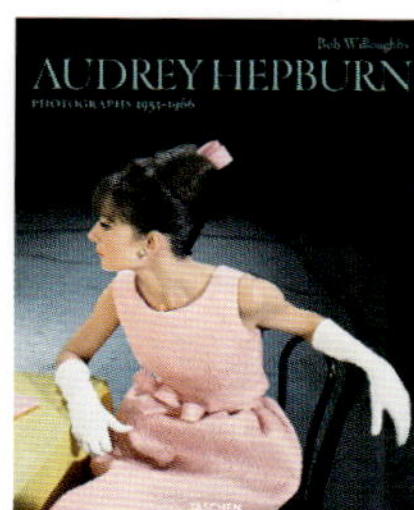

Er kam näher heran als alle anderen – der Studiofotograf Willoughby (1927 bis 2009) verfiel Audrey Hepburn in platonischer und fotografischer Liebe. Seine Bilder sind bis heute das intensivste Denkmal der zartesten Hollywood-Göttin.

This studio photographer got closer than anyone to Audrey Hepburn. Bob Willoughby (1927 – 2009) fell in platonic and photographic love with her, and his photos are still the most intensive commemoration of the gentlest Hollywood goddess.

Bob Willoughby, Audrey Hepburn,
Taschen, 49,99 Euro

MacLean

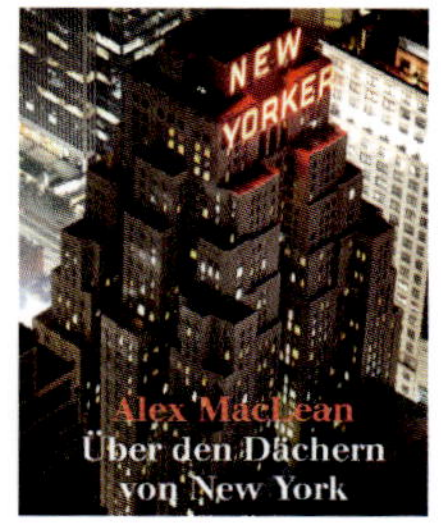

Es gibt ein New York, das man nur von oben sehen kann, das Dach-New-York mit seinen Parks, Pools, Gemüsebeeten, Baumschulen und sogar Tennisplätzen. Es ist ein geheimes New York, das der Flugfotograf MacLean detailliert wie nie zuvor zeigt.

There's a New York you can only see from the sky – rooftop parks, pools, vegetable patches, tree nurseries and tennis courts. It's a secret city that the aerial photographer Alex MacLean shows us in unprecedented detail.

Alex MacLean, Über den Dächern von New York,
Schirmer/Mosel, 49,80 Euro

Weinand

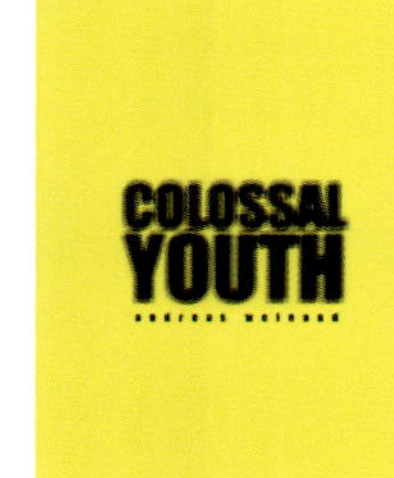

Sechs Jugendliche, die Jahre der Wiedervereinigung 1988 bis 1990 – Andreas Weinand hat in zwei Jahren eine der intensivsten und stärksten Studien über die elektrisierende Kraft, jung zu sein, fotografiert und zeigt, wie zeitlos der Gefühlstaumel der Jugend ist.

Six young people photographed from 1988 to 1990: Andreas Weinand has produced one of the most intensive and powerful studies of the energy of youth; and shows us how timeless the dizzy emotions of the young really are.

Andreas Weinand, Colossal Youth,
Peperoni Books, 25 Euro

Hoepker

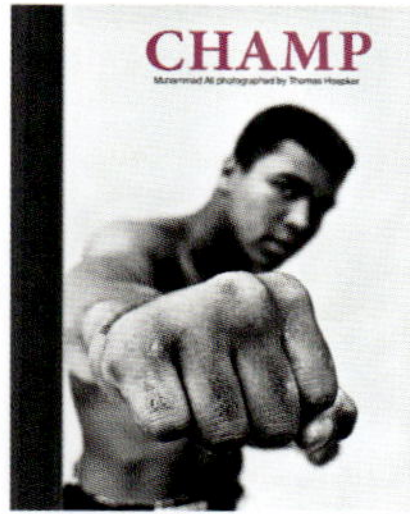

Der große Boxer und der Fotograf – über Jahre begleitete Thomas Hoepker den Champ Muhammad Ali und kam mit der Kamera faustnah und fühlbar an den Boxer heran. Auch wem Boxen egal ist, es sind die Fotos, die hier gewinnen.

A great boxer and a photographer: Thomas Hoepker followed Muhammed Ali for years and got palpably closer to him than virtually anybody else has done. And even if you aren't really interested in boxing, these photos will really knock you over.

Thomas Hoepker,
Champ, Peperoni Books, 36 Euro

Römer

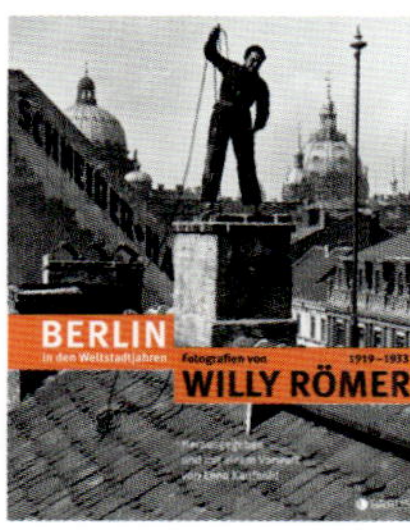

Einer der immer hinguckte – Willy Römer (1887 bis 1979) gehörte in der Weimarer Republik zu den wichtigsten Pressefotografen Berlins, und seine Bilder sind bis heute intensive und seh-süchtige Dokumente eines deutschen Alltags. Weil ja noch Frieden war.

Willy Römer (1887 – 1979), one of pre-war Berlin's most important press photographers, always looked that bit closer. Even today, his pictures are impactful documents of everyday German life in those still peaceful days.

Willy Römer, Berlin in den Weltstadtjahren,
Edition Braus, 39,95 Euro

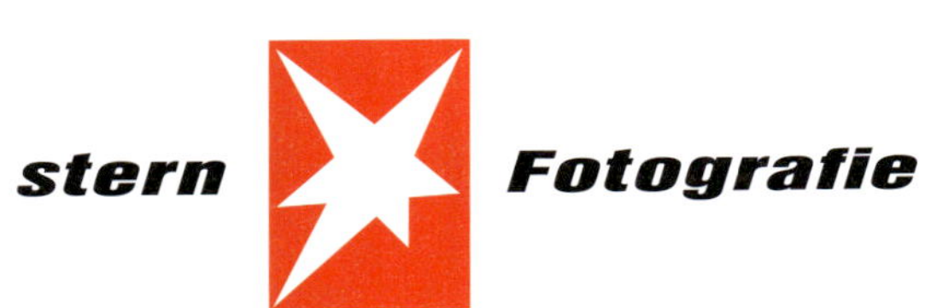

stern Fotografie

Das Portfolio zum Sammeln
Collect the international portfolio

Nr. 1
Christopher Pillitz
vergriffen

Nr. 2
Sebastião Salgado
vergriffen

Nr. 3
Hans-Jürgen Burkard
Bestellnr.: 70011052

Nr. 4
Konrad R. Müller
Bestellnr.: 70011065

Nr. 5
Peter Lindbergh
vergriffen

Nr. 6
James Nachtwey
Bestellnr.: 70010907

Nr. 7
William Klein
Bestellnr.: 70011420

Nr. 8
Herb Ritts
vergriffen

Nr. 9
Annie Leibovitz
vergriffen

Nr. 10
Michel Comte
vergriffen

Nr. 11
Nan Goldin
vergriffen

Nr. 12
Das Bild vom Menschen
Bestellnr.: 70010587

Nr. 13
Henri Cartier-Bresson
vergriffen

Nr. 14
Robert Lebeck
Bestellnr.: 70010519

Nr. 15
Bettina Rheims
vergriffen

Nr. 16
David LaChapelle
vergriffen

Nr. 17
Patrick Demarchelier
Bestellnr.: 70016950

Nr. 18
Sante D'Orazio
vergriffen

Nr. 19
Volker Krämer
Bestellnr.: 70016950

Nr. 20
Mario Testino
vergriffen

Nr. 21
Giorgia Fiorio
Bestellnr.: 70016949

Nr. 22
Bruce Weber
vergriffen

Nr. 23
Francis Giacobetti
Bestellnr.: 70016948

Nr. 24
Horst
Bestellnr.: 70016933

Nr. 25
Peggy Sirota
Bestellnr.: 70016935

Nr. 26
Peter Beard
Bestellnr.: 70016934

Nr. 27
Andreas H. Bitesnich
Bestellnr.: 70016947

Nr. 28
Ellen von Unwerth
Bestellnr.: 70016946

Nr. 29
Peter Lindbergh
Bestellnr.: 70016945

Nr. 30
Karl Lagerfeld
Bestellnr.: 70016944

Nr. 31
André Kertész
Bestellnr.: 70016943

Nr. 32
Rankin
Bestellnr.: 70016942

Nr. 33
Robert Mapplethorpe
Bestellnr.: 70016941

Nr. 34
Terry Richardson
Bestellnr.: 70037263

Nr. 35
Man Ray
Bestellnr.: 70037264

Nr. 36
Martin Parr
Bestellnr.: 70037265

Nr. 37
Anton Corbijn
Bestellnr.: 70037266

Nr. 38
Bruce Weber
vergriffen

Nr. 39
Elliott Erwitt
Bestellnr.: 70037637

Nr. 40
Cecil Beaton
Bestellnr.: 70037638

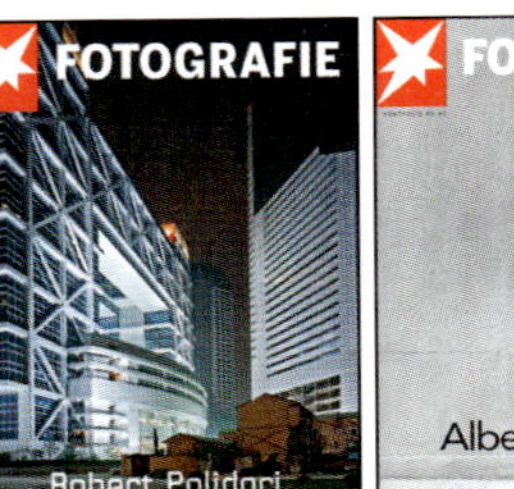

Robert Polidori
Nr. 41
Bestellnr.: 70037639

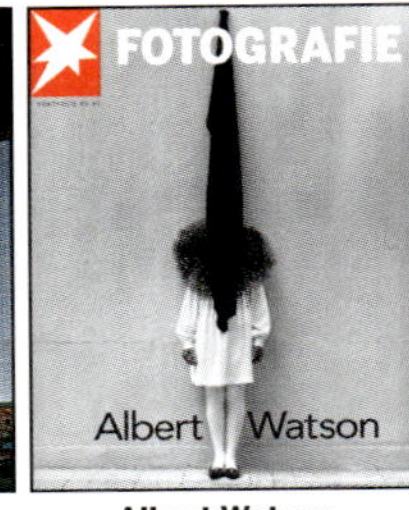

Albert Watson
Nr. 42
Bestellnr.: 70037640

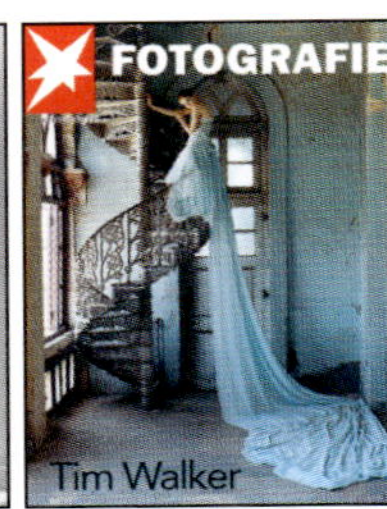

Tim Walker
Nr. 43
Bestellnr.: 70049845

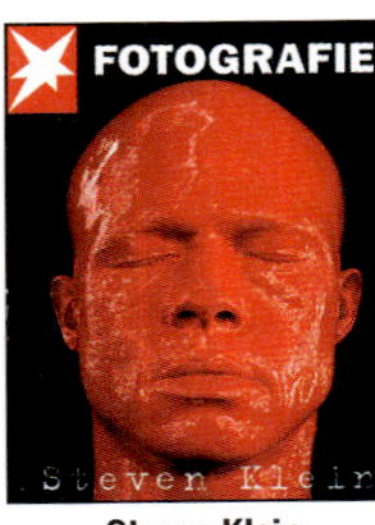

Steven Klein
Nr. 44
Bestellnr.: 70049846

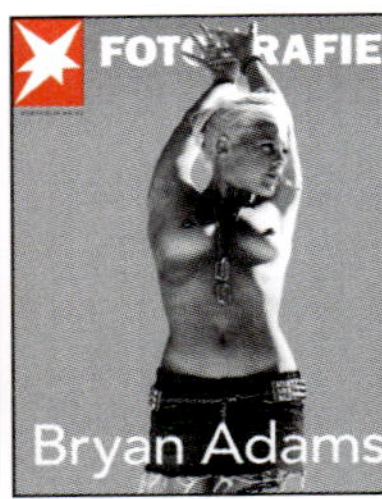

Bryan Adams
Nr. 45
Bestellnr.: 70049847

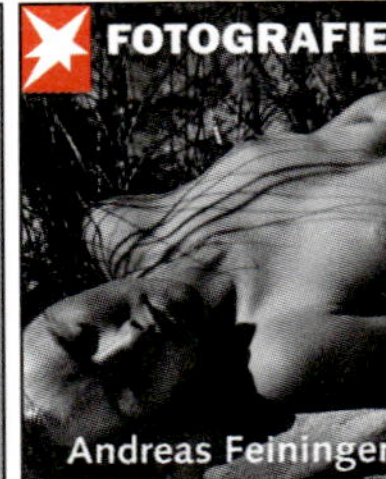
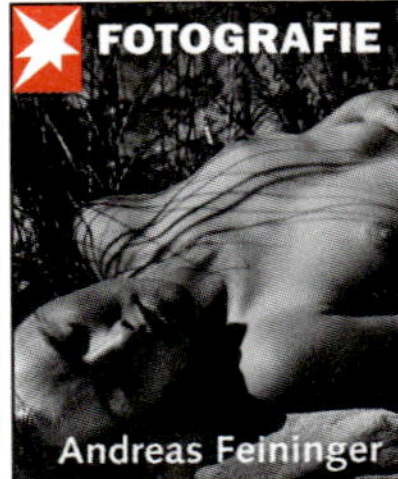

Andreas Feininger
Nr. 46
Bestellnr.: 70049848

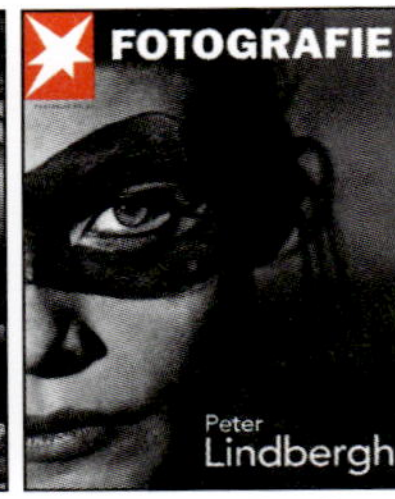

Peter Lindbergh
Nr. 47
Bestellnr.: 70050617

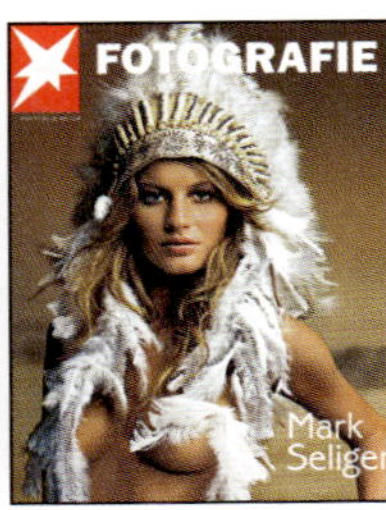

Mark Seliger
Nr. 48
Bestellnr.: 70050618

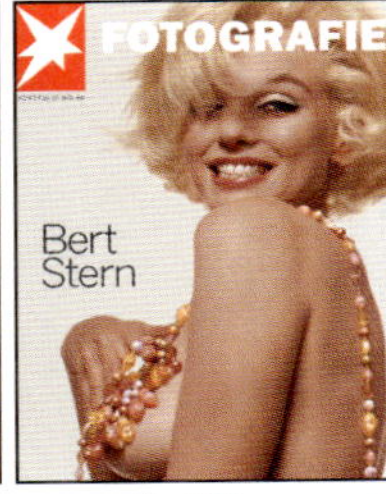

Bert Stern
Nr. 49
Bestellnr.: 70055396

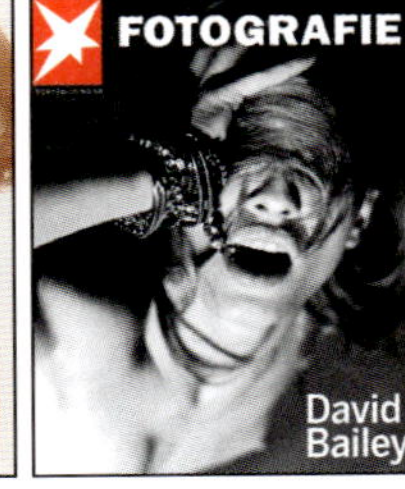

David Bailey
Nr. 50
Bestellnr.: 70055397

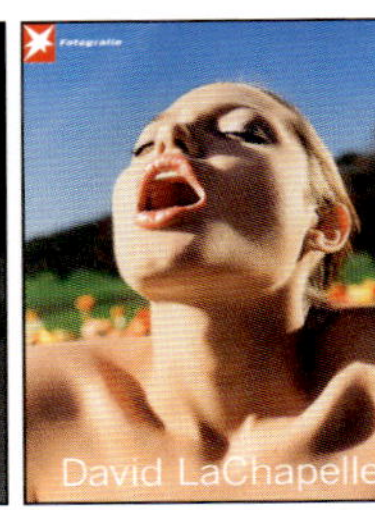

David LaChapelle
Nr. 51
vergriffen

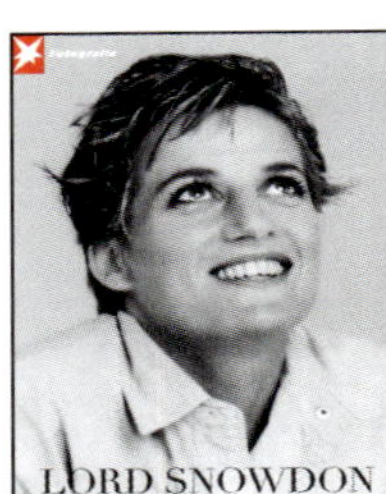

Lord Snowdon
Nr. 52
Bestellnr.: 70055399

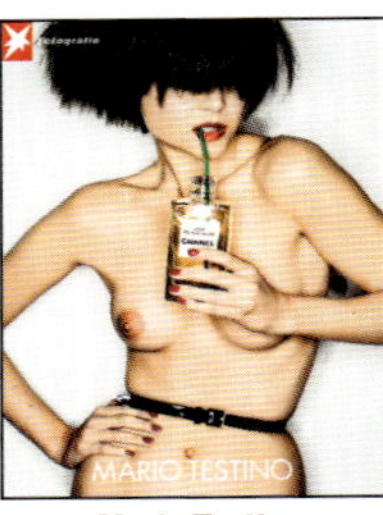

Mario Testino
Nr. 53
vergriffen

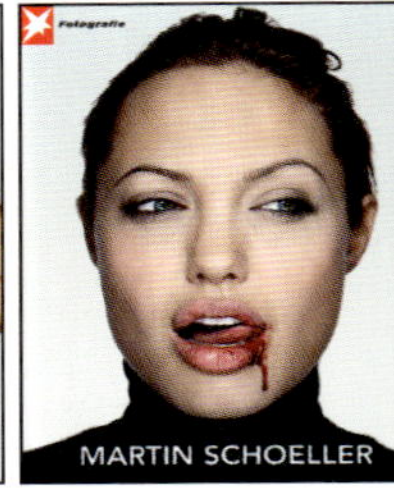

Martin Schoeller
Nr. 54
Bestellnr.: 70055401

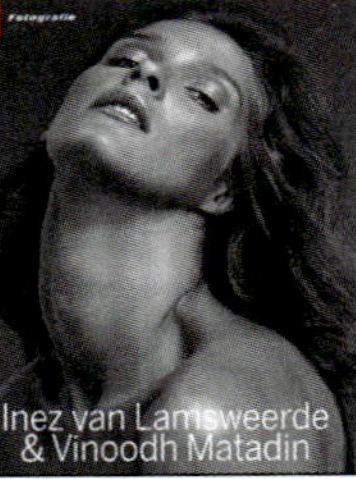

Lamsweerde & Matadin
Nr. 55
Bestellnr.: 70080172

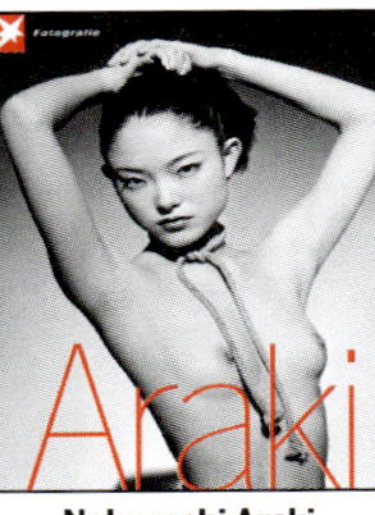

Nobuyoshi Araki
Nr. 56
Bestellnr.: 70080173

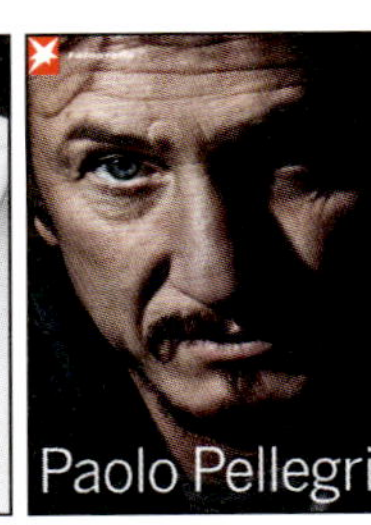

Paolo Pellegrin
Nr. 57
Bestellnr.: 70080174

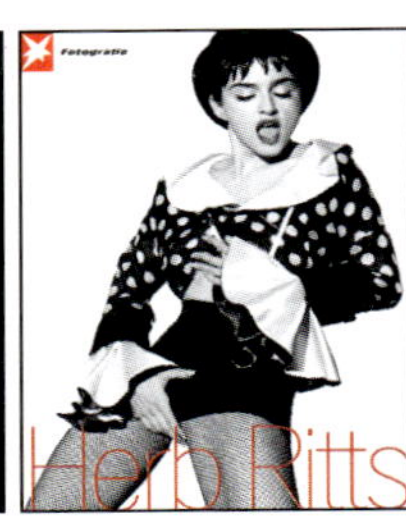

Herb Ritts
Nr. 58
Bestellnr.: 70080175

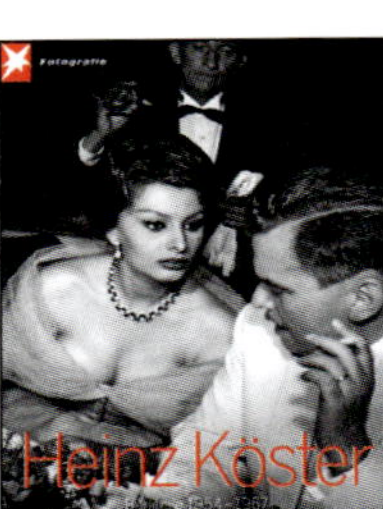

Heinz Köster
Nr. 59
Bestellnr.: 70092518

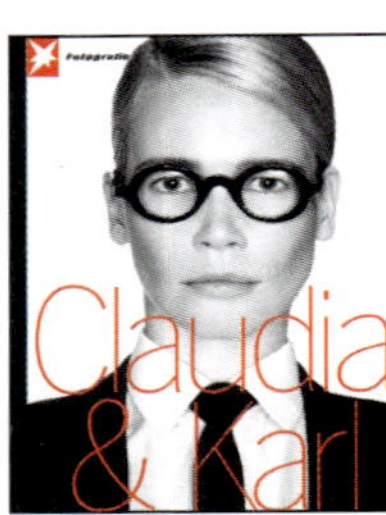

Karl Lagerfeld
Nr. 60
Bestellnr.: 70092519

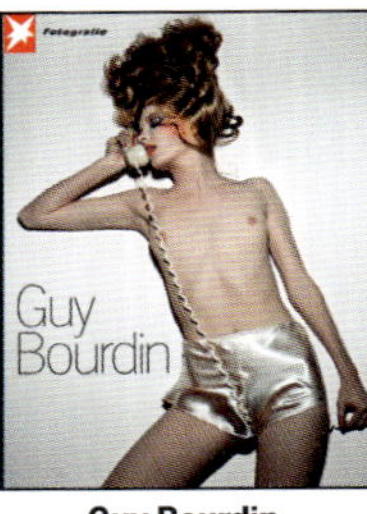

Guy Bourdin
Nr. 61
Bestellnr.: 70092520

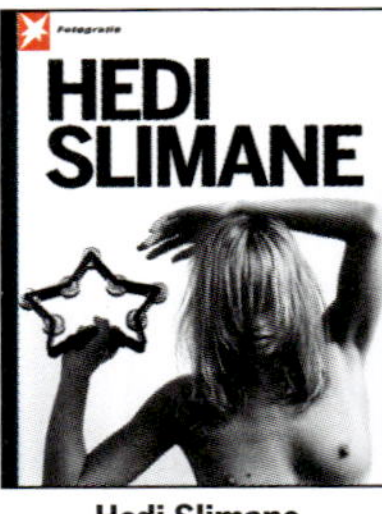

Hedi Slimane
Nr. 62
Bestellnr.: 70092521

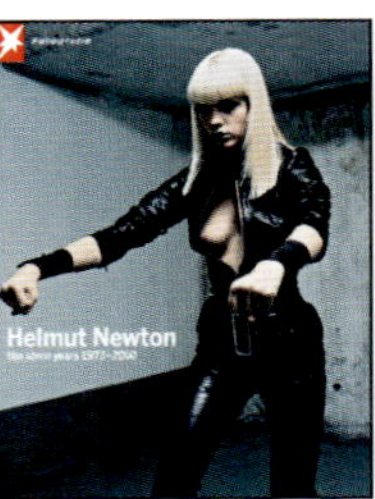

Helmut Newton
Nr. 63
Bestellnr.: 70108234

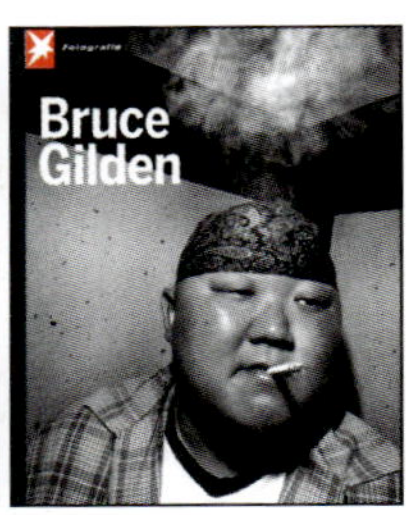

Bruce Gilden
Nr. 64
Bestellnr.: 70108235

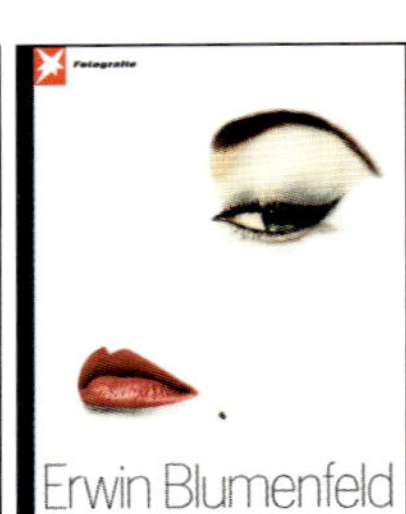

Erwin Blumenfeld
Nr. 65
Bestellnr.: 70108236

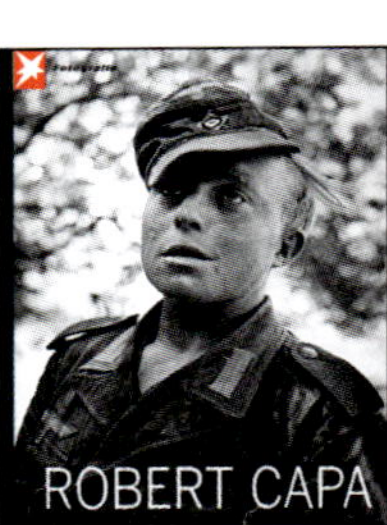

Robert Capa
Nr. 66
Bestellnr.: 70108237

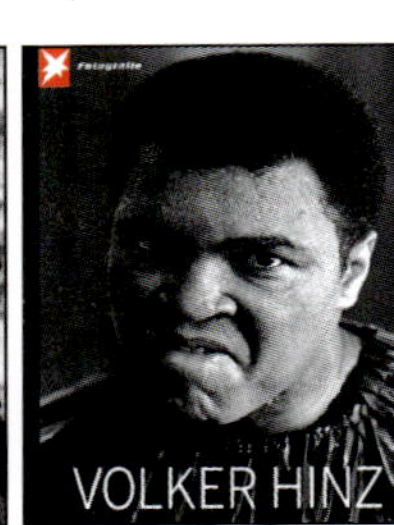

Volker Hinz
Nr. 67
Bestellnr.: 70135314

---

stern FOTOGRAFIE im Abo zum Sonderpreis von 15 Euro pro Ausgabe

Tel.: 01805/861 80 00. Bitte Bestellnummer 800227 angeben.

Fehlen Ihnen noch Ausgaben?

Bestellen Sie (noch lieferbare Hefte) zum Preis von 15 Euro bzw. 29,90 Euro für das Doppelheft Nr. 12, ab Heft 51 im Einzelverkauf 18 Euro (im Inland inkl. Versandkosten) bei: *stern*-Versandservice, 20080 Hamburg, Tel.: 01805/861 80 00, Fax: 01805/861 80 02, E-Mail: *stern*-Service@guj.de (Bestellnummer nicht vergessen).
Unsere Leser in der Schweiz wenden sich bitte an: *stern*-Leser-Service, Postfach, 6002 Luzern, Tel.: 0041/41/248 44 11, Fax: 0041/41/248 44 04

Subscribe to stern FOTOGRAFIE at a special price of €15 per book

Phone +49/1805/861 80 00 and quote the order number 800227

Missing any past editions?

You can order any book still in print for €15, €29.90 for the double edition No. 12, and €18 per book from Edition No. 51 (price incl. p&p to addresses in Germany): *stern*-Versandservice, 20080 Hamburg, phone: +49/1805/861 80 00, fax: +49/1805/861 80 02, e-mail: *stern*-Service@guj.de – please do not forget the order number.
Readers in Switzerland should contact: *stern*-Service Schweiz, Postfach, 6002 Luzern, phone +41/41/248 44 11, fax +41/41/248 44 04

Herausgeber: Thomas Osterkorn, Andreas Petzold **Design-Direktion:** Mark Ernsting **Bildnachweis:** Alle Fotos © Volker Hinz **CvD:** Andreas Projahn, Nicole Granzin **Gestaltung:** Susanne Söffker (verantwortlich), Jürgen Voigt **Redaktion:** Jochen Siemens **Textchef:** Petra Schnitt **Koordination:** Samira Meyer **Bildredaktion:** Andreas Kronawitt, Beate Magrich **Dokumentation, Lektorat:** Susanne Elsner, Hildegard Frilling, Christa Harms **Übersetzung:** Andrew Craston **Redaktionsanschrift:** *stern* FOTOGRAFIE, Am Baumwall 11, 20459 Hamburg **Verlagsleitung:** Thomas Lindner, Simon Kretschmer (stv.) **Herstellung:** Thomas Koch, Monika Hehlmann-Werner **Vertriebsleitung:** Marco Graffitti/DPV Deutscher Pressevertrieb **Anzeigen:** Heiko Hager, Sabine Plath **Reproduktion:** Peter Becker GmbH, Würzburg **Druck:** Mohn Media, Gütersloh. © *stern* Gruner + Jahr AG & Co KG, Hamburg. ISBN 978-3-652-00068-0/ISSN 1619-2656

Vertrieb im Handel/Distributed to the trade by: Deutschland: teNeues Verlag GmbH + Co. KG, Am Selder 37, 47906 Kempen, Tel.: 0049/21 52/916-0, Fax: 0049/21 52/916-111, E-Mail: books@teneues.de, www.teneues.com **Großbritannien und Irland:** PGUK Arts, 8 The Arena, Mollison Avenue Enfield, Middlesex EN3 7N Tel.: 0044/208/8040044 Fax: 0044/208/8040044, E-Mail: info@pguk.co.uk, www.teneues.com **USA:** teNeues Publishing Company, 7 West 18th Street, New York, N.Y. 10010, Tel.: 001/212/627-90 90, Fax: 001/212/627-95 11, E-Mail: tnp@teneues-usa.com, www.teneues.com **Frankreich:** teNeues France S.A.R.L., 39, rue des Billets, 18250 Henrichemont, Tel.: 0033/2/48 26 93 48, Fax: 0033/1/70 72 34 82, E-Mail: info@teneues.fr, www.teneues.com **Schweiz:** OLF S.A., Z.I. 3, Corminbœuf, 1701 Fribourg, Tel.: 0041/26-467 51 11, Fax: 0041/26-467 54 66, E-Mail: commandes@olf.ch, www.olf.ch

Danke an Henriette, Flora und Theodor. Und an all die Freunde und Kollegen, die diese Arbeit über Jahre möglich gemacht haben
Contact: prinzhinz@aol.com